PEPPER

PEPPER

A Guide to the World's Favorite Spice

JOE BARTH

ROWMAN & LITTLEFIELD
Lanham • Boulder • New York • London

Published by Rowman & Littlefield
An imprint of The Rowman & Littlefield Publishing Group, Inc.
4501 Forbes Boulevard, Suite 200, Lanham, Maryland 20706
www.rowman.com

6 Tinworth Street, London SE11 5AL, United Kingdom

British Library Cataloguing in Publication Information Available

Library of Congress Cataloging-in-Publication Data

Names: Barth, Joe, 1950–
Title: Pepper : a guide to the world's favorite spice / Joe Barth.
Description: Lanham, Mariland : Rowman & Littlefield, 2018. | Includes bibliographical references and index.
Identifiers: LCCN 2018026456 (print) | LCCN 2018031502 (ebook) | ISBN 9781442273931 (Electronic) | ISBN 9781442273924 (cloth : alk. paper)
Subjects: LCSH: Pepper (Spice) | Cooking (Pepper) | LCGFT: Cookbooks.
Classification: LCC SB307.P4 (ebook) | LCC SB307.P4 B37 2018 (print) | DDC 633.8/4—dc23
LC record available at https://lccn.loc.gov/2018026456

∞™ The paper used in this publication meets the minimum requirements of American National Standard for Information Sciences—Permanence of Paper for Printed Library Materials, ANSI/NISO Z39.48-1992.

Printed in the United States of America

CONTENTS

Preface

I FIRST BECAME INTERESTED IN PEPPER after reading Mark Kurlansky's *Cod: A Biography of the Fish That Changed the World*. Then after I read his book *Salt: A World History*, I began thinking about other everyday things we take for granted. Pepper had been staring me in the face for as long as I could remember, and yet I knew next to nothing about it. As I started reading about pepper, my interest was piqued and I began to research it in earnest. After a year or so, it was clear that a trip to Kerala would flesh out with experience what I had learned by reading. The adventure began on January 22, 2016.

The lengthy itinerary from Toronto to Kochi was subject to several unexpected delays and transfers. After a long car ride, my driver dropped me off at the Kairali Ayurevedic Spa Resort in Palakaad. I had arranged to meet Stephen Lynch, a colleague from my university who had just completed a consulting project in Tanzania. Stephen was no stranger to the Kairali Resort, and he convinced me that it was the best way to overcome the effects of jet lag. He was absolutely right. After five days of being pummeled twice daily by expert masseurs, taking yoga lessons, and eating special healing diets prescribed by the Ayurvedic doctor in attendance, I felt great. I remember seeing my first *Piper nigrum* plant just outside my cabin, resplendent with bright green leaves and heavy with pepper berries. No photographs could do it justice.

Sometimes serendipity is better than the best laid plans. After leaving the Kairali resort, we headed off to the house I rented on Bolgatty Island, not far from Fort Kochi and the historic spice trading area called Jew Town. The owner of the property, Dr. Joseph Mankiddy, dropped in and heard about my plan to write a book about pepper. A call to his friend Mr. Parathode Antony, an important landowner and entrepreneur in the town of Cheruthony, set up my first visit to a pepper plantation. Mr. Parathode introduced me to a local pepper trader, and we were able to follow the supply chain back to Jew Town. There, at the now defunct Pepper Exchange, we met Mr. Anand Kishore, the proprietor of Kuruwa Enterprises, one of the largest independent spice traders in Kerala. Mr. Kishore spoke with us at length about the spice trade and all its complexities.

I visited the oldest Synagogue in India, the Church where Vasco Da Gama was buried, the Dutch Palace, Hill Palace, and many other sites relevant to the historical section of this book.

The time passed all too quickly and I returned to Guelph to start writing this book.

Introduction

I F YOU ARE PASSIONATE ABOUT FOOD, food ingredients, and food provenance, then this book is for you. It is about the spice called pepper, made from the fruit of the *Piper nigrum* vine. Pepper is an ingredient found in every kitchen and as a condiment on virtually every dining table. It is used in the preparation of countless recipes and is sprinkled on foods as a condiment, often without much thought. It also plays a role in the preservation of certain cold meats, aspics, and pâtés. What is less known is that the essential oil of pepper is an ingredient in many popular perfumes and insect repellents, and it plays an important role in both traditional and modern medicine.

Despite the proliferation of this spice and its many uses, most people know very little about it: where it comes from; how to assess its quality; how long it can be stored; or, in some cases, even what it tastes and smells like. In fact, because pepper is so easy to use, knowledge about it is not essential for most people. Thousands of recipes include the phrase "salt and pepper to taste" with no particular regard for the intended level of contribution made by the pepper toward the flavor of the final dish. For most people, it is simply bought whole or ground and is added to food during cooking or as a condiment when the dish is served. Since knowledge can enhance your enjoyment and appreciation of many things, knowing more about this ubiquitous and surprisingly impactful spice may help you enjoy and appreciate the food you shop for, prepare, and eat more than ever before. To get you started, here are a few of the many facts about pepper found in this book.

- Four kinds of peppercorns are produced from the fruit of the same perennial evergreen vine.
- Stubbornly hard to grow, *Piper nigrum* evolved in India, a land known for its annual monsoon cycle. It requires 1.5–2 meters of rainfall each year, does not tolerate long dry periods, and needs 65 to 95 percent humidity, with average temperatures around 86°F (30°C).
- *Piper nigrum* is susceptible to a host of biological pests, including molds, which thrive in warm, damp soils, affecting roots and stems and sometimes producing metabolites with toxic properties in the fruit.
- *Piper nigrum* is best grown at elevations of 500–1,500 meters in forest loam soils that are rich in the nutrients needed. Strong breezes and good drainage are required to help keep the molds at bay.
- Peppercorns ripen unevenly over a period of six weeks and thus are unsuited to mechanical harvesting. Like many products from the tropics, such as coffee, tea, and cocoa, pepper is produced on the backs of the planet's working poor.
- Pepper was a key motivator in the exploration and colonization of the globe by the Spanish, Portuguese, Dutch, and English. Wars were fought and populations enslaved in order to secure ever more plentiful supplies of cheaper pepper.
- At the time of writing (2018), the price of pepper being traded is low ($4,300 US per ton), down substantially from a peak of $10,000 in 2013. Prices rose 310 percent from 2003 to 2013. The world demand for pepper is expected to grow from four hundred forty-six thousand tons in 2017 by ten thousand tons per year.
- Black pepper is the most common (and most traded) spice in the world. By some estimates, 34 percent of the world trade in spices is black pepper.

The Origins of Pepper

India lies between the Arabian Sea on the west and the Indian Ocean on the east, its southern tip extending to within a few degrees north of the equator. The vast Deccan Plateau stretches in a huge triangle from a few hundred kilometers north of Mumbai to Cape Comorin on the southern tip. A narrow, fertile strip of land from thirty to eighty kilometers wide runs between the plateau and the coast on each side, separated from the interior plateau by the Eastern and Western Ghats mountain ranges. These low-lying, worn, and ragged mountains eventually degenerate into hills in the extreme south. The Western Ghats are somewhat higher than those on the east, with peaks reaching an average height of one thousand meters, several over twenty-five hundred meters high. The western approaches can be quite steep, sometimes precipitous, with deep valleys, cascading waterfalls, and streams passing through the lush lowlands before draining into the Arabian Sea. The Ghats slope gently to meet the great inland plateau. It is one of the world's great biodiversity hot spots, home of wild elephants, tigers, lion-tailed macaques, sloth bears, and many plant and animal species found nowhere else. Although extensively peopled for thousands of years, virgin tropical rainforest still covers 20 percent of the region. Luxuriant forests of rosewood, teak, and sandalwood are dotted with rubber, coconut, and spice plantations.

The hot, wet climate makes such vegetation possible. Each year from June until September, strong southwest winds pick up moisture from the Arabian Sea before making landfall along the west coast of India. As the winds move the moisture-laden air to higher elevations, they discharge increasing amounts of rain. The coastal plains receive approximately fifty inches of rain a year, but the Western Ghats get at least three times that much. The region receives 90 percent of its annual rainfall during the monsoons—torrential downpours interspersed with periods of intense sunshine, swirling mists, and clouds. In Malabar, the southwest coast of India, the monsoons are so strong that sand dunes and waves have created picturesque backwaters, where huge quantities of rice are produced. Aquaculture has been practiced here for centuries. Shrimp, crab, giant gourami, and tilapia raised in shallow tidal ponds are exported throughout the world. Good, deep harbors are few, thus the area was isolated for centuries from the maritime trading routes found farther north.

Here, in the hot, humid jungles along the Western Ghats, *Piper nigrum* evolved to survive and prosper. Although there are many places with similar climates, and plant breeders have adapted the plant to those places, the pepper of the Malabar region of India is still considered the best pepper in the world.

What Is Pepper?

There are many spices called pepper, and consequently, the word *pepper* can be confusing in a number of languages. At the root of the confusion about which spice pepper refers to is that all have the quality of pungency, a highly desirable sensation in the enjoyment of food that humans have

sought for thousands of years. Since a great deal of the food we eat is insipid (neutral or mild tasting) in its natural form, the addition of salt, acids,
herbs, and spices—and in particular, pepper—makes food more interesting, appetizing, and enjoyable. The root of the word *pungent* is the Latin
verb *pungere*, which means to pierce, prick, or sting. As it pertains to the
taste of food, pungent means a strong, sharp taste or smell.

During the fourteenth and fifteenth centuries, a growing number of
lower-cost alternatives to pepper became available to add pungency to
food. In order to inform potential buyers about the use of these new
spices, the name *pepper* was given to many of them. Consequently, there
is a proliferation of spices called *pepper* and some confusion as to which is
which. In many languages, pepper refers interchangeably to various seeds
of the Piperaceae family of plants (including black, white, green, and red
peppercorns, long pepper, spiked pepper, cubeb pepper). However, *pepper*
also refers to the pod-like fruit of the capsicum family of plants (collectively
called chili peppers) and several other biologically unrelated spices, such as
Sichuan pepper, mountain pepper, melegueta pepper, and hepper pepper,
to name just a few.

The definition of pungency and the sensation of pungency have influ-
enced meanings attributed to the word *pepper* beyond its original usage as
a proper noun. *Pepper* is used as a verb to describe the acts of sprinkling
(for example, "the Spanish language is peppered with English words");
striking ("he peppered the advancing forces with small arms fire"); and
inundating with repeated requests ("the boy peppered his uncle with
endless questions"). As an adjective, it means sharp or stinging (as in a
peppery speech) or hotheaded and irascible (a peppery leader). Germans
have attached additional meanings to the word *gepfeffert*, ("peppered" in
English) to describe high prices or scandalous (spicy) stories. The SPICE
Channel, a soft pornography channel carried by many cable TV companies, illustrates the semantic connection between sex, heat (pungency),
and spice.

Given the confusion about the name of many spices called pepper,
along with the rich breadth of meanings attached to the word as an adjective, adverb, or verb, it is useful to explore what actual pepper from the
Piper nigrum plant (the subject of this book) is and what it is not. First, we
will describe spices called pepper that are not the subject of this book,
beginning with plants completely unrelated to the Piperaceae family of
plants. After that, we will move onto spices that come from the same family of plants and conclude with a description of peppercorns from *Piper
nigrum*, the subject of this book.

Meet the Peppers

Chili Peppers

One of the most common overlaps in the word *pepper* is between the pod-like fruits of the *Capsicum* genus of plants (hot pepper, chili, paprika, cayenne, aji) and peppercorns made from the seeds of the *Piper nigrum* vine that belongs to the Piperaceae family.

Capsicums are plants familiar to most people as brightly colored bell peppers[1] (which are not pungent at all), as well as an incredible variety of "hot" chili peppers, such as the well-known jalapeño, habanero, cubanelle, scotch bonnet, cayenne, and others. Within the genus *Capsicum*, there are twenty-seven species, five of which have been extensively cultivated. Hundreds (if not thousands) of *Capsicum* cultivars have been discovered in the wild or hybridized by professional and amateur botanists. Even though the cultivated plants tend to be larger or fleshier than those found in the wild, many plant breeders and aficionados do not see the wild varieties as inferior. New varieties of chili peppers are still being found in Central and South America, and the living genetic material (called germplasm) is being maintained in collections throughout the world. *Capsicum*s are perennial plants that will produce fruit in the first year of growth and thus are grown as an annual in cool, temperate climates. In order to extend the growing season, new chili pepper plants are started indoors and moved outside after all risk of frost has passed. In tropical climates, the same capsicum plant will produce fruit for several years.

*Capsicum*s are native to the Americas. The first *Capsicum* seeds to reach Europe were scattered in a churchyard in the town of Baiona Pontevedra in Portugal, site of the first landfall by Columbus's returning ship *Pinta* in 1493. Since many capsicums are strongly pungent, most people at that time referred to them as peppers to reflect its use an ingredient with pungent characteristics. The English (*pepper*), Dutch (*peper*), Spanish (*pimiento*), and Portuguese (*pimentão*) words for pepper are the same whether it refers to capsicum or peppercorns from the *Piper nigrum* plant. Several other European languages differentiate between peppercorns and capsicum: German (*pfeffer* vs. *paprikaschote*), French (*poivre* vs. *poivrons*), Italian (*pepe* vs. *peperoncino*). Fortunately, many *Capsicum*s are now called chilies, reducing some of the confusion about what is real pepper.

After its introduction to Europe in 1493, *Capsicum annum* (one of the twenty-seven species of the *Capsicum* genus) became a popular decorative garden plant with pretty, colored fruits that was also used as a cheap, locally grown ingredient to add pungency to food. The royal families of Portugal and Spain who financed Columbus's voyages of discovery did not encourage *Capsicum* planting, because it could easily be grown in most European climates and would displace revenue from the importation and sale of pepper. Capsicum seeds were widely disseminated and plants appeared in southern France, England, Turkey, the Balkans, and as far away as India within a relatively short time. By 1570, *Capsicum annum* were grown in large quantities in Turkey and Hungary, where they were particularly well adapted to local conditions.

The Hungarians learned to preserve the *Capsicum* they grew by drying and grinding them into a powder called paprika. After harvest, the peppers are matured for a few weeks before washing, drying, and grinding. The mill master determines the quantity of seeds to be ground with the pepper pods, to produce the desired level of pungency and color in the paprika. There are eight grades of paprika, in part determined by the quality of the fruits after harvest.

First-quality fruits are used to make the top four grades (special, capsaicin-free, and two kinds of delicatesse). Second-quality fruits are used to make lower grades of paprika (fine sweet, semi-sweet). Fruits from later harvests and those rejected from higher grades are used for rose, while spotted fruits not belonging to any other grade are used for pungent, which is the lowest grade. The crushed capsicums are heated during the grinding process to release the oil in the seeds. The oils react with the pigment to produce the characteristic deep red color. During the grinding process, if the fruits are heated too much, they will scorch. If they are not heated enough, the moisture content will be too high and both the flavor and color will be affected.

Paprika powder is long lasting in storage, easy to use, and available all year long. The Hungarians, occupied by the Ottoman Turks from 1541–1699, also produced dried red pepper flakes called *pul biber* (some-

Table 1.1. Paprika Grades

Grade	Color	Pungency
Special	bright, fiery red	none to very little
Capsaicin-free (mild table)	bright red	none, some bitterness
Delicatesse (table)	bright red (darker or light)	barely detectable
Delicatesse (hot table)	bright red (darker or light)	less pungent
Fine Sweet	dark or yellowish red	less pungent
Semi-Sweet	darker to yellowish red	pungent
Rose (pink)	dull red to pale yellow	markedly pungent
Pungent	light brown to green	very pungent

times called *Aleppo pepper*), often seen today in shakers on the tables of Italian restaurants. Hungarian cuisine has a strong association with the iconic *chicken paprikash* dish, flavored and colored with the paprika spice. Spain also began production of paprika and differentiated their product, hence the Spanish and Hungarian paprika types still sold today.

Chili peppers are used fresh, dried, or processed into chili oil, pastes, and hot sauces. Tabasco, in continuous production since 1868, is the earliest known commercial brand of hot sauce made from *Capsicum frutescens*, considered by some to be a variant of *capsicum annum*, the original plant species imported by Columbus. Sriracha sauce, a capsicum-based hot dipping sauce originally from Thailand, has become very popular in recent times. Sriracha was named Ingredient of the Year for 2010 by *Bon Appétit* magazine. Thousands of brands of hot sauce (many of them independent, small producers) are on the market for fans of hot, spicy foods to choose from. A notable difference between capsicums and peppercorns is aroma: Capsicums have almost no aroma, despite their often profoundly sharp taste.

Monk's Pepper (Vitex agnus-castus)
Monk's pepper is a tree native to the Mediterranean area that grows well in southern England and the northeast coast of the United States (Nantucket, Long Island, etc.). Grown in cool climates, it has delicately textured, aromatic foliage and spikes of lavender-colored flowers that attract butterflies in late summer. Monk's pepper is not a spice or seasoning but has pharmacological properties. The leaves, seeds, and delicate shoots have an anaphrodisiac effect, hence the name "monk's pepper" or "chasteberry."

Grains of Selim (Xylopia aethiopica)
Grains of Selim are also known as Kimba pepper, African pepper, Moor pepper, Negro pepper, Kani pepper, Kili pepper, Senegal pepper (*Poivre de Sénégal*), Ethiopian pepper, and Hwentia. Grains of Selim are sometimes called Guinea pepper, but Guinea pepper is a confusing term also used in reference to Ashanti pepper and melegueta pepper (grains of paradise).

Xylopia aethiopica is an aromatic evergreen tree that can grow up to twenty meters tall in humid coastal areas or river plains throughout tropical Africa. The wood is widely used for construction of houses and boats because it is resistant to termite attack. The fruit (a pod, containing seeds, somewhat like a bean pod) is used to season soups and stews and to make Café Touba, a very popular beverage in that part of the world. Café Touba is produced by mixing grains of Selim, cloves, and other spices with the green coffee beans during roasting. Grains of Selim are produced by smoking the green (unripe) seedpods giving them a sticky consistency. The pod contributes nutmeg, resin, and camphor or eucalyptus notes to the coffee's aroma. It has a bitter, pungent flavor.

Grains of Paradise (Aframomum melegueta)

Also known as melegueta pepper, ossame, and, confusingly, Guinea pepper, *Afromomum melegueta* is an herbaceous perennial plant belonging to the ginger family that grows in the wetlands of Nigeria, Ghana, Guinea, and Liberia along the West African coast. Colorful reddish-orange, tear-shaped pods five to seven centimeters long contain sixty to one hundred small, irregularly shaped reddish-brown seeds used as a substitute for black pepper, with hot, spicy, cardamom flavor notes. The fresh seedpods are eaten whole on São Tomé Island in the Gulf of Guinea, where they are called ossame.

Grains of paradise became readily available in Europe when Fernão Gomes, a Portuguese merchant, was granted a monopoly on trade along the West African coast by King Alfonso of Portugal in 1469. The popularity of grains of paradise declined in Europe as black pepper and other spices became more broadly available. *Capsicums* brought back by Columbus were sometimes named *malagueta* (*mala fide* = bad faith, or attempt to deceive) pepper. After Vasco da Gama discovered the sea route to India in 1496, vastly increased supplies of black pepper further reduced the demand for melegueta pepper.

Grains of paradise are common in the cuisines of West Africa, and remain an important component in the production of some craft beers (particularly in Belgium), Holland gin, and Akvavit. The traditional cuisines of Denmark, Iceland, and other Scandinavian countries still employ grains of paradise, although it is not clear why that is so. Grains of paradise are described as having a light, clean aroma, blossom sweetness with some coconut, cardamom, and pungent flavors.

Alligator pepper, Mbongo spice, hepper pepper, or African cardamom (Aframomum danielli, also known as bastard melegueta)

A close relative of grains of paradise is the seeds and seedpods of *Aframomum danielli*, *Aframomum citratum*, or *Aframomum exscapum*. Called by a variety of names, *A. danielli* is grown in the same area as *Aframomum melegueta*. Alligator pepper gets its name from the seedpods, which bear a resemblance to the skin of an alligator, and each pod contains a bottle-shaped seed that is used as a spice in ways similar to grains of paradise.

Mountain Pepper, Cornish Pepper Leaf, Tasmanian Pepper Berry (Tasmannia lanceolata)

Also known as pepper bush, *Tasmanian lanceolata* is a plant unrelated to *Piper nigrum* and native to cooler parts of southeast Australia and Tasmania. It can be grown in many temperate environments, including southern England where it exhibits as a garden plant. It is shrub-like, growing to a height of two to ten meters, with black, two-lobed berries appearing in the autumn. Both the leaves and dried berries were used at one time as a substitute for black pepper by colonial settlers. Mountain Pepper is grown commercially and exported to Japan where it is a flavoring ingredient in wasabi production. It is also sold as a bush food condiment to fans of indigenous foods found growing wild in the outback. The pungency of mountain pepper comes from a compound called polygodial. Polygodial has strong antimicrobial, antifungal, and antioxidant properties that are useful to inhibit food spoilage. It is a potent medicinal agent used to treat *Staphylococcus aureus* and *Candida albicans* infections. Dorrigo pepper (*Tasmannia stipitata*) is similar.

Sichuan Pepper, Japanese Pepper, Sancho Pepper, Chinese Coriander (various Xanthothylum, including X. Simulans; X. Bungeanum, and X. Piperitum)

Sichuan pepper belongs to the citrus family of plants.[2] Sichuan pepper is not pungent but rather induces a numbing, tingling, galvanic (metallic) sensation on the tongue. Sichuan pepper plants are known as the "toothache tree" in Chinese folk medicine in recognition of the plant's ability to numb pain. In China, Sichuan pepper is one of the components of five-spice powder. It is an important ingredient in the cuisines of Nepal and Bhutan because it is one of the few weather-hardy spices that grow in the region. Sichuan pepper is available as an oil as well as a ground spice. Batak or Andaliman pepper from Samosir Island in Sumatra is similar.

Pink Pepper, Peruvian Pepper, American Pepper, Brazilian Pepper (Schinus molle; Schinus terebinthifolius)

Pink pepper is the fruit of an evergreen tree native to the Peruvian Andes that grows well throughout parts of North and South America. Only the female tree has berries. The dried berries are sometimes combined with black pepper for their color rather than taste. It is the source of a strong, resilient wood traditionally used to make saddles and thus has been introduced throughout many parts of the world. The leaves and berries of the *Schinus molle* tree are toxic and potentially harmful to poultry, pigs, calves, and young children. The FDA does not consider it to be generally safe for humans, although in small amounts (such as its use as a condiment) it is not known to be harmful. The Brazilian pepper tree, *Schinus terebinthifolius*, is an invasive species in Bermuda, Florida, and Hawaii that is spread by birds who eat the berries and spread the seeds. It is in the same family as poison ivy and must be handled with care to avoid a similar skin reaction. A respiratory irritant is released when burned, making disposal by incineration hazardous.

Water Pepper, Marshpepper Knotweed (Persicaria hydropiper)

Persicaria hydropiper is a temperate-zone annual that grows to a height of seventy centimeters in wet, marshy areas around the world. The domesticated plant leaves are used as a vegetable in Japan. The wild variety is much more pungent than the domesticated cultivars and can be used to make a sauce by soaking in vinegar with a small amount of cooked rice. It has a bitter/pungent taste due to rutin (bitter) and polygodiol content (also found in grains of paradise). The wild variety produces oils that cause skin irritation, much as nettles do.

Meet the Pipers

Piperaceae is a family of plants related to *Piper nigrum* that have culinary, medicinal, and pharmacological uses. In the next section, we will explore some of these, beginning with important plants that do not bear the pepper name but belong to the same family of plants.

Betel Leaf (Piper betle)

Betel leaves come from a perennial climbing vine similar in appearance to *Piper nigrum*. It originated in the Indo-Malayan region. Betel plants are seldom found in the wild but are extensively cultivated in India, Bangladesh, Pakistan, Sri Lanka, Malaysia, and Indonesia. Betel leaves are chewed (together with lime, betel nut, or tobacco) for its stimulant and psychoactive effects. Betel leaf is not to be confused with the betel nut, the fruit of the areca palm (*Areca catechu*). Betel leaves, betel nut, lime, and tobacco are sold as an addictive, somewhat carcinogenic preparation called paan. Not all paan is addictive or carcinogenic, for example, *paan masala*, often provided as a breath freshener in Indian restaurants, is unlikely to contain areca nut, betel, or tobacco.

Kawa (Piper methysticum)

Kawa is a native of the South Pacific Islands, and it contains a narcotic drug widely used by the people of that region. *Piper methysticum* means "intoxicating pepper." It is a perennial shrub with broad, heart-shaped leaves that thrives in climates similar to where *Piper nigrum* grows. The active component (kavalactone) is found in the roots (15 percent), stumps (10 percent), and basal stems (5 percent). Medicinally, kavalactone can be used to promote lactation in females who have recently delivered a child. Pacific Islanders use the roots of the plant for making the potent beverage called Kawa-Kawa. Kawa-Kawa played important roles in their social and religious ceremonies such as the celebration of marriage and birth, mourning death, curing illness, and removing curses. Its pharmacological effect is non-intoxicating (it does not dull mental processes), but it is a narcotic that induces a euphoric state of tranquil well-being that eventually leads to a deep, dreamless sleep. Kava can also be consumed by chewing. *Piper excelsum*, the New Zealand variety (also known as *Maori Kawa*) has no narcotic properties.

Pepper from the Piper (Piperaceae) Family of Plants

Piperaceae are a family of plants within the major group of flowering plants called angiosperms. Piperaceae are perennial climbers, producing small clusters of fruits called drupelets. Drupes are fleshy fruits with thin skins and a central stone or seed, such as cherries, plums, peaches, and olives.

Cubeb Pepper (Piper cubeba)

Mostly grown in Java and Sumatra, cubeb pepper (also known as Java pepper and tailed pepper) is a perennial climbing vine with round branches three millimeters thick and adventitious roots appearing at the joints, similar in appearance to the *Piper nigrum* vine. Cubebs are often cultivated using coffee trees as an armature to support the vine. Unlike black peppercorns, cubebs have a completely straight, short stalk (petiole) attached to each berry and many of the seeds are hollow. They are harvested by hand prior to full ripeness and then dried in the sun. The wrinkled pericarp (outer skin) varies in color from gray-brown to black. The aroma of cubebs is described as agreeable and the taste as persistent, pungent, acrid, with eucalyptus or camphor-like notes in the aroma. Cubeb pepper has been described as tasting slightly bitter, something like allspice, or like a cross between allspice and black pepper. Cubebs, although in plentiful supply, are rarely seen in North American or European spice shops.

From the seventh century onward, cubebs were available in Europe from Arab traders as one of a number of exotic spices. By the Middle Ages, cubebs were a popular lower-cost alternative to black peppercorns until the price of peppercorns began to decline in the seventeenth century. Rumored to be an aphrodisiac and fertility aid, cubebs were widely used during the Middle Ages for the treatment of lack of appetite, chronic bronchitis, gonorrhea, oral and dental diseases, fever, bad breath, infection, and even demonic possession!

Cubebs are used ground or crushed as a spice. They are the primary flavoring agent in Sauce Sarcenes, dating back at least as far as fourteenth-century England. Sauce Sarcenes is sweetened almond milk thickened with rice flour, spiced with cubebs, saffron,[3] ginger, and mace. In Moroccan cuisine, cubeb is used in savory dishes and in *markouts*, little diamond-shaped pastries made of semolina with honey and dates. Cubebs appear in the list of ingredients for the famed spice mixture *ras el hanout* and in Indonesian curries.

Cubebs are sometimes a flavoring agent in the production of gin (notably the Bombay Sapphire brand). Cubebene (the essential oil of cubebs extracted by steam distillation) is used to flavor cigarette and smokeless tobacco products. It was the forerunner of the modern menthol cigarette. Until World War II, cubeb cigarettes (popular brands like Marshall's, Dr. Perrin's, and Recqua's) were sold in pharmacies for the treatment of asthma, head colds, hay fever, and other respiratory problems. Cubeb dolls were popular during the late nineteenth and early twentieth centuries. Some of these dolls were used much like an incense burner to release the aroma of cubeb cigarettes into a room. Edgar Rice Burroughs, the famous fiction author of the Tarzan, Barsoom, and Pellucidar books, was fond of smoking cubeb cigarettes. He humorously quipped that if he had not smoked so many cubebs, there might never have been Tarzan. In 2001, the Swiss flavoring firm Firmenich isolated Cubebol (also found in basil), which is used as a freshener in chewing gum, toothpaste, and other products.

Cubeb pepper has a long history of falsification and adulteration. It is sometimes adulterated with *Cubeb baccatum* (aka the climbing pepper of Java). Cubeb essential oil is sometimes adulterated with *Cubeb crassipes* (aka false cubeb), and oil of patchouli is sometimes adulterated with cubeb oil. Cubeb pepper has a complex chemistry, but it does not contain piperine, the prime source of pungency found in black pepper.

Ashanti, Benin, Uziza, West African Pepper (Piper guineense)

A close relative of cubeb pepper, *Piper guineense* is also known as West African pepper, Ashanti pepper, Benin pepper, Uziza pepper, and false cubeb. It is sometimes called Guinea pepper; however, the name Guinea Pepper is confounding, because the grains of paradise (*Aframomum melegueta*) and grains of Selim (*Xylopia aethiopica*) are often called by the same name. *Piper guineense* vines are native to topical regions of Central and Western Africa and grow up to twenty meters in length, climbing up trees by means of roots that extend from the nodes of the plant (adventitious roots). They are semi-cultivated in countries such as Nigeria, where the leaves are used to flavor stews. *Piper guineense* is easily recognized. The dried berries are noticeably smaller and smoother than cubeb pepper and have a reddish color; also, the petioles (tails) are distinctly curved. *Piper guineense* pepper tastes similar to cubeb pepper but is much less bitter and has a fresher, herbaceous flavor.

Voatsiperifery Pepper (Piper borbonens)

Voatsiperifery peppercorns are three-millimeter-long ovals with a tail of five or six millimeters. The head is somewhat smaller than cubeb pepper with a longer petiole. Indigenous to Madagascar, voatsiperifery (also known as tsiperifery pepper) is one of the world's rarest spices from the Piperaceae family of plants. Production is less than fifteen hundred kilograms per year. It is not commonly available in North America or Europe. Voatsiperifery is a vine that climbs up the tall trees of the humid tropical forests. Berries grow on branches that are ten to twenty meters above ground, and they are harvested manually from June to September. Production is very limited because unlike cubeb pepper, it grows only in the wild and is dangerous to harvest. Voatsiperifery is less spicy than cubeb or black pepper, with distinctive ginger, citrus/lemon flavors. It has been described as having a strong, resinous aroma with pine forest notes.

Indian Long Pepper (Piper longam); Indonesian Long Pepper (Piper retrofractum)

The Indian and Indonesian types of long pepper are very similar. *Piper longam* is a flowering vine that climbs up armatures (either tall poles or trees) to a height of three meters above ground. If plenty of space is available, they can also be trained to grow along cordon catch wires strung between posts parallel to the ground to make harvesting easier. It is a good intercrop between banana or fruit trees because *Piper longam* can tolerate up to six hours of full shade daily. Long pepper is a robust plant that is resistant to disease, and thus is much easier to cultivate than *Piper nigrum*.

The stems and roots are used as a stimulant in Ayurvedic medicine. Unripe fruiting spikes (2.5-centimeter-long catkins) are harvested and sun dried for use as a spice. Long pepper tastes similar to black pepper but is more pungent (hotter). Long pepper contains piperine, the same source of pungency found in peppercorns. Long pepper, almost unknown in European or American cuisines, is relatively common in Indian and Nepalese vegetable pickles, some North African spice mixtures (Moroccan *ras el hanout* and *felfla harra*), and in Indonesian and Malaysian cooking. It is available in North America and Europe from Indian grocery stores, where it is known as *pippali*. The ancient history of black pepper is often interlinked (and confused) with that of long pepper. Pliny erroneously believed black pepper and long pepper came from the same plant. Both long pepper and black peppercorns were known to the Romans and early Europeans, but by the fourteenth century, black pepper had completely displaced it.

Long pepper fruits (dried) and roots are among the most important medicinal plants used in the Indian systems of medicines—Ayurveda, Unani, and Sidha. An infusion of immature fruits and roots in hot water is used for the treatment of chronic bronchitis, cough and cold, palsy, gout, rheumatism, and lumbago. The fruit and roots are used as antidotes for snakebite and scorpion sting. The fruit is a vermifuge and is useful after childbirth to check post-partum hemorrhage. The fruit is also used as a sedative in insomnia and epilepsy, as an agent to discharge bile and gall bladder obstructions, and as an abortifacient.

Black, White, Green, and Red Peppercorns (Piper nigrum)

Although the name *Piper nigrum* suggests that the spice from this plant is black, four different kinds of peppercorns are produced from the same plant, depending on when the fruits are harvested and how they are processed. Each of the four kinds of peppercorns contributes to the taste and aroma of food differently. The pepper berries go from a bright green (immature, unripe) to yellow (mature, ripe) and finally a bright red color (fully mature and overripe). As the pepper berries ripen over a six-week period (February–March), aroma peaks early in the process and then declines as the volatile aromatic oils are lost to the atmosphere. The aromatic oils are

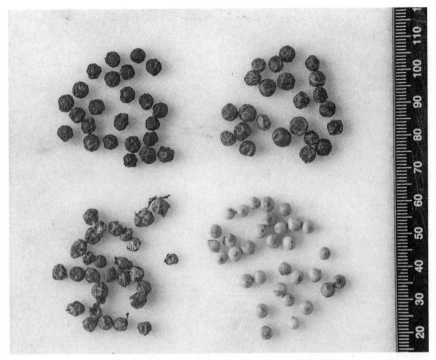

Photo 1.1. Clockwise from lower left: Green, black, red and white peppercorns. Simon Day

concentrated in the pericarp, or fleshy skin surrounding the seed inside. During the same period, the pungency increases continuously as the berries achieve full maturity. Piperine (the molecule responsible for pungency in peppercorns) is concentrated in the seed and is maximized as the fruit becomes overripe and bright red in color.

When berries are picked at the green stage, the aroma is peaking, but the pungent taste in the seed is less developed. Consequently, green pepper is highly aromatic with a fresh, lighter flavor. In places where it is grown, green peppercorns are often used right off the vine in season. Green peppercorns are preserved for future use by freezing whole, drying in the sun, freeze-drying, or pickling to prevent fermentation of the pericarp, where the aromatic oils are found. Frozen green pepper is made simply by freezing the berries. Even though Europe is the major importer of frozen green pepper, it is almost unknown in North American markets.

Dehydrated (dried) green pepper has the green color and the flavor of fresh pepper. After soaking in water, the dried berries become full and soft, but do not have the texture of fresh green pepper berries. Freeze-drying

Photo 1.2.   Green peppercorns in brine; pepper oleoresin. Simon Day

ensures better dehydration. Dried green peppercorns can be found in Indian and Chinese specialty stores or from internet suppliers. Some people prefer the taste of the freeze-dried green peppercorns from Brazil to the less expensive sun-dried product from India; however, aficionados seek out the pickled variety. Pickled green pepper is available canned in a brine solution or in small jars containing a brine and vinegar mixture that preserves the natural color and texture of the berries. Pickled green peppercorns are expensive due to the increased processing costs; however, they are perfect for dishes where a strong pepper aroma should be achieved without an overpowering pungent taste (for example, pepper cream sauces used on fish). To overcome the disadvantages of the poor texture and weak flavor of dried green pepper and the high unit weight and packing cost of canned and bottled green pepper, cured green pepper has been developed. Berries are thoroughly cleaned in water, steeped in saturated brine solution for two to three months, drained, and packed in suitable flexible polyethylene pouches.

Berries destined to become black pepper are picked just before they turn yellow. The time of harvesting is important because it affects the balance of aroma and pungent taste. The well-developed pericarp retains a good amount of the fragrant aromatic oils, while the almost fully developed seed contains an ample amount of piperine to provide pungency. In order to retain the aroma, it is very important to prevent the pericarp from fermenting and detaching itself from the seed within. Berries are briefly immersed in boiling water to kill off any naturally occurring yeasts and bacteria, then dried in the sun. If there is plenty of sunshine and low humidity it is also possible to dry them rapidly without the hot water bath. When dried, the pericarp turns a dark brown/black color that is fully attached to the seed within.

If the berries are harvested somewhat later, the pericarp may begin to detach from the seed, resulting in mostly black peppercorns with a proportion of visible white seeds and fragments of broken black pericarp. If the proportion of white peppercorns is small (less than 4 percent), it will be sold in the spice trade as peppercorns. Poor-quality black pepper, as indicated by the presence of excess white peppercorns, often has a bitterness in its taste profile. Pepper with a larger proportion of the white seeds is destined to become ground pepper or used to produce pepper oleoresin, a concentrated pepper extract for industrial food production use.

White peppercorns are produced from mature, bright red fruits. At this stage, a little aroma is left; however, the seeds contain high concentrations of piperine. The berries are de-fruited by a process called *retting*. Berries are immersed in water for several days, where naturally occurring yeasts and bacteria degrade the pericarp. Then the fruits are agitated by foot (much like traditional port wine production) and washed to dislodge and remove any remaining bits of pericarp. When no pericarp remains, the seeds are dried. White pepper is used when a strong pungent taste is needed. White pepper tastes hotter than black pepper but is less complex, with fewer flavor notes and less aroma. It is common in Chinese, Vietnamese, and Scandinavian recipes. White pepper is sometimes used for aesthetic reasons, to avoid visible black flecks in white sauces and mashed potatoes. Due to the additional processing costs, white pepper is more expensive than black pepper.

Fully mature, somewhat overripe red berries are strongly flavored but low in aroma. Similar to green peppercorn processing, red peppercorns must be sun dried rapidly, freeze-dried, or pickled before the ripe pericarp ferments and detaches from the seed within. Most red-colored peppercorns sold in stores are Sichuan pepper, the product of the *Zanthoxylum simulans* or *Zanthoxylum bungeanum* trees, and is completely unrelated to red peppercorns. True red peppercorns are unusual in North American markets, and production primarily takes place in Cambodia.

Some peppercorns are named according to the region of production. Malabar, the world's original black pepper, comes from the southwest coast of India. Malabar pepper is moderately hot, aromatic, and pungent tasting. Most of the generic black pepper sold is a mixture from a variety of other, cheaper sources and should not be confused with Malabar pepper, widely acclaimed to be the best pepper in the world.

Tellicherry is the namesake of modern-day Thalasseri, a city on the southwest coast of India just north of Cochin. Tellicherry pepper does not come from Tellicherry: it refers to a family of special grades of black pepper that encompasses the largest and highest-quality peppercorns from the Malabar region. Tellicherry pepper is harvested at the same time as ordinary black pepper. It has a complex aroma with hints of cedar, flowers, and cherries and a more robust taste. Tellicherry has received the coveted Protected Geographical Indication status that defines the region of production precisely and protects the name from being used by other producers from other regions.

Sarawak is a state of Malaysia located in the northwest corner of Borneo Island. In the local language, it is called land of the hornbills, after the rhinoceros hornbill, Sarawak's state bird. Commercial production of pepper is deemed to have started in 1884 when a duty was first levied on pepper exports from Sarawak. Plantation farming had begun about twenty years earlier. There were some efforts made to encourage Chinese migrants to take up pepper production by making land available.

Sarawak is famous for its high-quality white pepper. Sarawak white pepper is a large, flavorful peppercorn with a uniform creamy-white color and hot flavor. The Malaysian Pepper Board has encouraged the production of Sarawak black pepper in recent years, and growers use rapid harvesting and forced-air drying methods to improve the quality. Sarawak black pepper is a medium-size pepper sometimes described as fruity with hints of chocolate and licorice. Sarawak is also the home of Rimbás pepper, grown along the river of the same name.

Lampung (also known as Lampong) black pepper comes from the southern tip of the island of Sumatra. Part of Indonesia, Lampung is the province where it has been produced since the fifteenth century. Lampung peppercorns are smaller than average and hotter than the black pepper from Sarawak. It is described as having citrus-lemon, woodsy, pine needle notes in the aroma. Lampung pepper is widely sold in the UK.

On the western shore of Sumatra, Banka Island is home to Muntok pepper, named after the principal port from where it is shipped. Muntok pepper is a widely distributed white pepper that is of good quality and affordable in comparison to Sarawak white pepper. It is distinguished by its eucalyptus and menthol notes in the aroma and a pale biscuit color. There are concerns that Muntok pepper plantations are at risk from tin mining activities. About 60 percent of the land formerly used to grow pepper on Banka Island has been taken over by tin mines that offer land owners higher profits in the short term. In addition to rendering the land useless for pepper cultivation, polluted water and radiation exposure of the people who live there threaten pepper production.

A number of former French colonies (Indochina) produce excellent peppercorns that are much touted by French chefs. Vietnamese and Kampot pepper hail from the former Indochinese colonies of France. Kampot pepper comes from Cambodia. During the Khmer Rouge regime, much of the pepper production ceased and has only recently become available again in any commercial quantity. Kampot pepper received Protected Geographical Indication Status (PGI) from the EU on February 18, 2016, and holds the ECOCERT certification. All types of pepper—green, black, white, and red—are produced in this region. Kampot peppercorns are larger than average, with guava and eucalyptus notes in their fragrance. Kampot red peppercorns, made from fully ripened fruits, are famous for having a powerful, fruity aroma combined with some residual sweetness.

Another former French colony, Madagascar produces pepper that is mild, with a smoky, charred oak-barrel aroma. Madagascar is a leading producer of green peppercorns that are pickled in brine and packed in cans. It is also the home of tsiperifery (aka voatsiperifery) pepper, the world's rarest and most expensive spice from the Piperaceae family of plants.

With the exception of Vietnamese peppercorns (which are exported everywhere), most of the production of the former French colonies is exported to France. Vietnam has become one of the world's major pepper producers in recent years and produces peppercorns of average size with notable lemon/citrus notes in its aroma and a strong, sharp, biting taste.

Originally a German colony, Cameroon (located in West Africa) was divided between France and England under the reparations at the conclusion of World War I. Both English and French remain official languages in Cameroon, even though it has been independent since 1971. Pepper was first planted in the Penja valley in 1958 by a French banana farmer named Antoine Decré. The first crop of Penja pepper consisted of a single forty-kilo bag of white peppercorns. White Penja pepper has a distinctive barnyard aroma. The pepper plants grow in volcanic soil that is very rich in minerals. Combined with an equatorial climate, the pepper plants thrive in the near perfect balance between rainfall and sun. Both black and white pepper is produced. Penja pepper rapidly became a favorite among Michelin-star chefs and commands very high prices. Currently, only three hundred tons of peppercorns are produced annually.

Pepper was introduced to Brazil as early as the seventeenth century; however, commercial production did not begin until 1933 in the northern states of Para, Maranhao, Espirito Santo, and Bahia. Brazil was the last country in the world to abolished slavery (1888). Part of the legacy of slavery was the immigration of agricultural workers, which peaked from 1931–1936, with over 72,600 immigrants from Japan alone. At that time, there was substantial pressure on the coffee growers to reduce costs, because of worldwide overproduction. Japanese immigrant workers were poorly treated and looked for alternatives to working on coffee plantations for unsustainably low pay. Other crops offered better opportunities. It is widely believed that a shipload of Japanese laborers stopped in Singapore where a horticulturalist purchased some pepper plant cuttings from a local market and took them to Brazil. The plants thrived and the peppercorns were found to be of very good quality. The *Cingapura* (named after Singapore) cultivars are highly disease resistant and require less agrichemicals than pepper grown in Vietnam and elsewhere.

Pohnpei, formerly called Ponape or Ascension Island, is part of Micronesia. Pohnpei produces small amounts of very high-quality pepper with a distinctive sweetness. It is considered one of the best peppercorns in the world. Unfortunately, local government interference in the privately held pepper industry in the late 1990s reduced production from over 100,000 pounds per year to less than 10,000 pounds. Production and supplies continue to be limited and erratic.

Throughout history, black peppercorns were the preferred spice, and the many substitutes described in this chapter were used only when the real thing was unavailable or unaffordable. The only rival to the popularity of black peppercorns is the chili (pod) pepper. A near obsession, possibly driven by the release of endorphins when consumed, exists among fans of ever-hotter chili pepper cultivars and preparations. This book will take you on a voyage of discovery that will forever change the way you think about pepper. It has been a driving force in the colonization of the Far East, the subjugation of entire populations, and wars fought between privately held companies who sought to monopolize its production and trade.

Pepper from Ancient Times to the Middle Ages

2

I T IS HARD TO BELIEVE THAT ordinary black pepper found on nearly every table in the world was a major force in the history of the world. Pepper was one of the first commodities that spawned global trade on a massive scale. Why pepper? It would keep for ten years or more, was light in weight, easy to transport, and at one time was worth the same as an equivalent weight of gold. Because pepper consists of many small peppercorns,[1] trade was easy to transact with precision. Unlike precious metals (gold and silver), coins, and bank notes, pepper was inherently useful beyond being a means of exchange: it made food taste good. Most people were able to enjoy pepper throughout history despite its extraordinary value: a single peppercorn was enough to flavor someone's meal.[2] Beyond all these reasons, consumers were simply obsessed with it. There were many substitutes available to add pungency to food, but despite being significantly lower in cost, none of them presented a desirable alternative to the real thing. Although for centuries it was difficult to procure, the development of long-distance transportation technologies changed everything. Beginning in the sixteenth century, pepper became increasingly available at progressively lower prices. Despite plentiful shipments, demand continued to be strong, just as it is today. The history of pepper is very much a story of exploitation: exploitation of the consumers, who wanted to buy pepper so badly they would pay almost any price, and exploitation of the growers and the enslaved people they needed to produce it. The history of pepper is the story of powerful people and rulers who sought to enrich themselves by controlling production of and trade in pepper. It is the story of conflict: private and state-sponsored wars, piracy, and colonialism. It is laced with woe, subjugation, and evil doing. However, the story of pepper is also a story of discovery, the evolution of ocean navigation, and the development of international finance and trade.

The use of pepper as a seasoning for food is obvious: you need only to look at recipe books, kitchen spice drawers, and dining tables to find it. Pepper has always been a remarkable foodstuff in that it has negligible nutritional value yet is widely sought after. It is not a significant source of fats, proteins, carbohydrates, vitamins, or minerals.[3] Indeed, it is fortunate that humans can survive very well without it because for millennia only the inhabitants of the Indian subcontinent had pepper. The rest of the world's people did not even know it existed.

Less obvious than the culinary were the therapeutic uses of pepper in Ayurveda (traditional Indian medicine), traditional Chinese medicine (TCM), and the medical practices of ancient Greeks and Romans.[4] Egyptians used it for embalming corpses to prevent putrefaction and collapse of the nasal passages.[5] Pepper could also be used to preserve food, especially cooked meats.

Once introduced to people in other parts of the world, pepper became an obsession. People would go to great lengths and great expense to obtain it, and thus it became a commodity that was bought, sold, or traded for tremendous profit. The farther from its source, the higher the price became. The ancient supply chain was long, arduous, dangerous, and complicated. Pepper made its way to Europe following a network of indirect routes, each cargo under the ownership and care of a different trader. Some pepper came overland, some by sea, or by a combination of land and sea routes. Not until the sixteenth century would ships transport pepper all the way from the source to its final destination. Each segment of the journey had its own hazards—robbers, pirates, enemy powers, storms, droughts, floods, starvation—calamities of every kind. Despite the risks, pepper trade profits substantively outweighed the risks. Along the way, each trader took a profit, resulting in peppercorns that ultimately were worth as much as the same weight in gold.

Pepper in the Ancient World

Much of what we know about ancient history comes from archeological finds; Assyrian and Arab inscriptions; and the writings of classic historians, geographers, and so-called natural philosophers, who were often the medical men of the day. The use of pepper in ancient health practices (such as Ayurveda or traditional Chinese medicine) persists today in some modern cultures. The earliest physical evidence of the medicinal use of pepper is the so-called Ebers Papyrus, dated around 1550 BCE. It consists of 110 pages and is over twenty meters long. It was discovered in 1874 by Georg Ebers, a German Egyptologist working in Thebes, and is kept in the collections of the University of Liepzig library. Considered one of most important ancient Egyptian medical documents, it contains specific references to pepper.

Some books have been available throughout recorded history, repeatedly translated, reproduced, and reissued. For example, the writings of Paracelsus, Julius Caesar, Pliny, and the Bible and Qur'an are more broadly available today than they were when initially written. From ancient writings and archeological evidence, we know that a brisk trade in spices was already taking place in 1200 BCE. At that time, the Mineans had established themselves in the southern part of the Arabian Peninsula, what is modern-day Yemen. Their capital city, Haram, was located several hundred kilometers from the coast, high along a desert strip in the mountains. The Minean homelands were mostly desert, with limited amounts of arable land. However, the Mineans were located at the nexus of several caravan routes between Gaza and Medina and thus came to rely on trading for much of their economy. In 950 BCE, the Sabaeans (located south of the Mineans) became the dominant civilization of the area, and they too prospered by trading spices. The Sabaean lands, which at one time encompassed modern-day Somalia, Ethiopia, Eritrea, and Yemen, were more fertile than the Mineans' territory and benefitted from irrigation made possible by the construction of an extensive system of dams, cisterns, and underground aqueducts called *qanats*,[6] some of which still exist as ruins today.

The Bible is an important source of information about the ancient kings of the region. The Queen of Saba (also known as Makeda, the Queen of Sheba) traveled to visit King Solomon (Suleiman in Arabic) in Jerusalem with gifts of spices, gold, and precious stones (I Kings 1:10). Solomon gave her "all her desire, whatsoever she asked" (1 Kings 10:13). "She left satisfied," implying that there was a sexual relationship. Some scholars believe that Menelik I, the King of Ethiopia, was the son of the Queen of Sheba and Solomon. Without doubt, the visit included the formalization of a relationship between the two kingdoms, including the adoption of early Judaic belief systems. Solomon was a spice trader, too. He built a number of fortresses to safeguard caravan passages through the southern and northern parts of his lands, which now encompass much of Jordan, Israel, and the western portion of Syria.[7]

An informal series of caravan routes (now called the Silk Road) evolved during this time, connecting the East with the West overland. Individual traders would band together for mutual protection and support as they crossed the continent. While people from many ethno-racial groups were involved in the pepper trade, Arabs and early Judaic people controlled most of supply chain. Small amounts of pepper reached Western Europe, which was in a primitive state of social evolution by comparison. Transported over long distances, pepper passed from one trader to another many times before reaching the consumer.

Transport over land was not the only way pepper made its way to the Middle East. Ancient mariners sailed along the coast in open vessels to the Red Sea, Persian Gulf, and Arabian Sea as far as India. Galley slaves propelled the early ships, assisted by sails only when the winds were favorable. Coastal navigation was the rule. Frequent stops along the shore were required to replenish supplies of food and water to sustain the rowers, which could number more than two hundred individuals. It would be many centuries before the compass, knowledge of wind patterns, and other navigational technologies enabled men to proceed with certainty beyond the visible shoreline for any length of time.

Coastal navigation made it easy for Sabaeans (who were located at the nexus of land and sea transportation) to establish control on trade in the region by preventing vessels from passing through the Bab-el-Mandab except under close supervision and the payment of tolls. The importance of this thirty-kilometer-wide strait between the Red Sea and the Gulf of Aden continues to this day, with sixty ships passing through every day on their way to or from the Indian Ocean.

The Arab-dominated spice trade carried on for centuries until 326 BCE, when Alexander the Great extended Greek dominance to India, having conquered most of the countries of the Mediterranean basin as far east as the Persian Empire (Iran). Alexander was not content with conquering so much of the world's known landmass at that time: he wanted control of the sea routes as well. The admiral of his navy, Nearchus, established new ports along the shoreline from northwestern India to the Persian Gulf. Here, too, ships needed to pass through another strategic narrows, the Straits of Hormuz. The Straits of Hormuz (fifty-four kilometers wide) is on the way from the Gulf of Oman to the Persian Gulf. With the land on both sides under Greek control, all ships were subject to paying taxes for safe passage. The sea routes were relatively safe from pirates, there being no land base available to them. Goods would be transferred to caravans at the headwaters of the Persian Gulf and proceed overland to Eastern Europe through areas under Alexander's control. This new route enabled a substantial amount of pepper to bypass the Sabaeans' strategic hold of the Red Sea route and thus increase the supply of pepper transported to Eastern Europe and the Mediterranean basin. Despite the increase in supply through the Persian Gulf, demand for pepper was so strong that neither the Greeks nor the Sabaeans suffered significant losses.

Some exotic luxury items like frankincense and myrrh originated in the Arab homelands, but most spices (including pepper, cinnamon, cloves, ginger, and nutmeg) were from India, Java, and as far away as China. Early Chinese and Javanese navigators sailed along the coasts of Asia, hopping from island to island, collecting and discharging cargoes of tradable goods as they went. Within a relatively short span of one hundred years after Alexander the Great, Arab and Chinese sea routes connected Egypt with China. Arab dhows sailed along the coast of the Arabian Sea as far as Sri Lanka.[8] Indian dhows traveled eastward from India as far as Malacca (the Spice Islands), where they met Chinese junks.[9] Some of these Chinese junks traveled as far west as Sri Lanka.

Trade was so important that between 285 and 246 BCE the Egyptian king Ptolemy II Philadelphus reconstructed an ancient canal originally dug by Darius in 487 BCE that connected the Nile in Egypt with the Red Sea, creating a sea route all the way to the Mediterranean.[10] The port city of Alexandria (named after Alexander the Great) on the Mediterranean coast of Egypt was the place where Greek traders met with Arab, African, and Asian merchants to acquire supplies of spices.

A number of kingdoms rose to power, flush with finances from trade. These kingdoms all came into being, prospered, and waned when the Roman Empire emerged as the next great world power.

Rome began as a town about 600 BCE. Primarily by force of arms, Rome progressively incorporated towns and villages that had been largely self-governing. In time, it governed the entire Italian peninsula. Most historians take the view that the Roman Empire officially began when Rome expanded beyond the Italian peninsula in 300 BCE, a few years after Alexander the Great's death in 323 BCE. Rome's formidable military had been land based. They developed a naval force in order to take modern-day Sicily away from the Carthaginians in the first Punic War (261 BCE). After that, Romans were accomplished sailors as well as foot soldiers. The Roman Empire reached its peak in 117 CE, when it encompassed the entire Mediterranean basin (including Egypt, the Levant,[11] Iraq, and parts of Iran), most of Europe (including all of France, the western part of Germany, and Britain as far north as Scotland). The so-called Roman peace

(*Pax Romana*) had the effect of creating a huge market for all kinds of traded goods, including pepper.

In 45 CE, Hippolus, a Greek sailor, discovered the biannual pattern of monsoon winds that enabled sail-powered ships to leave the ancient Egyptian port city of Ocelis (on the Bab al Mandeb across from the Sabaean shores) in the spring and arrive at the Malabar coast in southern India in forty days. The Roman supply of pepper was immediately enhanced. In the autumn, the pattern of winds reversed, allowing an equally speedy return from India. The short transit times and small crews made it possible to take sufficient food and water aboard sailing ships to cross the Indian Ocean without following the shore. Substantially lower costs led to a dramatic increase in trade between the India and the Roman Empire and effectively ended the Arabian spice trade monopoly for the next four centuries.[12]

Pliny the Elder provides written evidence regarding the amount of pepper used by the Romans (77 CE): "There is no year in which India does not drain the Roman Empire of 50 million sesterces" (roughly equivalent to $75 million US today). Although pepper was very popular among Romans, it had all the hallmarks of an obsession. Pliny goes on,

> It is quite surprising that the use of pepper has come so much into fashion, seeing that in other substances which we use, it is sometimes their sweetness, and sometimes their appearance that has attracted our notice; whereas, pepper has nothing in it that can plead as a recommendation to either fruit or berry, its only desirable quality being a certain pungency; and yet it is for this that we import it all the way from India.[13]

Archeological evidence that the Romans used large quantities of pepper was found at two of the extreme outposts of the empire in Oberaden[14] (Germany) and Vindolanda[15] (England, forty kilometers west of Newcastle on Tyne near Hadrian's wall), where legionnaires were posted to repel the attacks of barbarian tribes. Special warehouses called *horrea piperataria* were constructed to store pepper and other spices in dry, dark conditions. Ruins of horrea have been found in sites throughout the Roman Empire, and several examples have been restored to near-original condition.[16] Aside from the use of pepper as a seasoning, pepper was a cure-all, much like modern-day aspirin. Dioscorides (40–90 CE), a Greek physician in the Roman army, wrote an extensive dissertation about the pharmacology of plants. He notes that pepper is effective as a warming agent, for curing problems of the urinary tract and digestive system, eye problems (cataracts), poisonous snake and insect bites, birth control, as an abortifacient, and elimination of white areas of the skin, among others.[17]

The Roman Empire had many problems in the third century CE. It was ungovernable by a single emperor in the face of military threats on two fronts, civil wars, a weak economy, and a vast territory. The Emperor Diocletian reorganized the Roman Empire by dividing it into parts. In 330 CE, his successor, Constantine, continued by designating Rome the capital of the Western Roman Empire and Byzantium (modern-day Istanbul) the capital of the Eastern Roman Empire. After his death, Byzantium was re-named Constantinople in his honor. Byzantium had been a Greek colony, and although Latin was the official language, Greek was spoken widely. Christianity was the dominant faith, and the Eastern Orthodox religion has its roots in Constantinople. Many historians refer to the Roman Empire after the fall of Rome in 496 CE as the Byzantine Empire. The Byzantine Empire lost Egypt and the port of Alexandria in 621 CE, effectively bring-ing the European domination of the trade in pepper to a close. However, despite setbacks, the Byzantine Empire enjoyed a robust economy and indulged in many luxuries for a few centuries before Constantinople fell to the Ottomans in 1493 and became known as Istanbul.

The Dark Ages

With the fall of Rome, Europe entered the Dark Ages, also called the me-dieval period (400–1450 CE). It was a time of decentralization of govern-ment and society. A decline in the population and movement of people from cities and towns into the countryside took place. The universal language, Latin, fell out of use; libraries were lost; roads fell into disrepair, making travel difficult; and famine, starvation, and plague appeared and reappeared for more than five centuries. The so-called barbarian states in Gaul (the Franks) and Germany (Ostrogoths, Visigoths, etc.) came into being, and feudalism replaced the Roman system of government. The rise of an extensive structure of wealthy nobles in the newly fragmented Western European region and the prosperity of Byzantium increased the demand for pepper. Pepper became a sign of wealth and power. Nobles proudly exhibited their prosperity by wheeling out massive amounts of pepper and other spices during banquets. Recipes were developed to use ever-larger amounts of spices from the Far East for purposes of conspicu-ous consumption. Pepper took the place of currency for many transac-tions: it was the common denominator among a profusion of monetary systems and could be stored for many years with its value remaining stable over time. Counted out one peppercorn at a time, pepper was useful for making small transactions.[18]

The Carolingian period, ending with Karl der Grosse (Charlemagne) in 949 CE, saw the establishment of kingdoms (Lombardy, Italy, Francia, Aquitaine, Bohemia, and Bavaria, among others) in what was previously the Western Roman Empire. Many modern-day European regions can trace their history, culture, and borders to the Carolingian period. One of the characteristics of the Carolingian rulers was their division of their lands more or less equally among their heirs. This practice inevitably created smaller and smaller states, resulting in frequent military activity between rival heirs and neighbors. It also set the stage for centuries of arranged marriages and marriages between relatives in order to consolidate the fragmented holdings of families in power. The Catholic Church played an important role in these activities in order to sustain its own wealth and influence. They alone could sanction incestuous marriage arrangements.

The Arab world had adopted the Islamic faith and once again became the critical link in the supply chain of pepper. Despite disruption of world politics and religious differences, the Arabs needed European markets, the well-to-do wanted pepper, and the spice traders needed supplies. During most of the medieval era, trade flourished in the Indian Ocean basin, and demand for pepper throughout Europe and the Mediterranean grew.

In order to protect their near monopoly, Arab traders were very secretive about the sources of their spices. The Arabs fostered and encouraged the mystique surrounding spices by a program of misinformation that persisted for centuries. They created fantastic stories about strange creatures that were hazardous to men and lived at the far ends of the Earth, where spices are grown. It was a brilliant strategy. These tales accompanied the spices, becoming ever more fantastic, as they were retold by one trader to another. The stories made pepper more exotic and fascinating to consumers, who would pay higher prices given the exceptional provenance obtained from their supplier. Simultaneously, these stories discouraged travelers and adventurers from trying to find their source: danger and death were thought to be certain outcomes from such a venture.[19]

Christianity was not predisposed to trading as an honorable way of life. Life in the medieval era was composed of three distinct groups: clergy, nobility, and peasants. The clergy and peasants considered merchants to be those who sought to enrich themselves at the expense of society without producing any of the goods they sold. The clergy convinced the peasants that merchants were evil and acted against God's will. Occasionally finding themselves under threat of persecution, merchants banded together into guilds (today these would be associations or cooperatives). The merchant guilds wanted to negotiate with the nobility (who wanted pepper and other luxury goods from the Far East) and gain credibility with the peasants (who also wanted, but could ill afford, the same things). Several guilds were associated with the spice trade, including pepper. The Pepperer's Guild of London, eventually becoming the East India Company, is an example. Members of the guild policed each other with codes of practice to ensure that weights were accurate, new stock was not mixed with old, and that the pepper was not adulterated with other materials to increase the weight. They guaranteed quality by garbling (inspecting, cleaning, sorting, and grading the pepper). Widespread cheating in the pepper trade resulted in laws making it a serious legal offense, and belonging to a guild implied that the buyer could expect honest trading.

Islam had a rather different view of merchants. They valued merchants (the Prophet Muhammad himself was a trader and caravan guide), and wealthy Muslim cities created an enormous demand for exotic luxury goods that only merchants could provide.

Relationships between Christians and Muslims were rocky at best. Nine crusades (1056–1292) spearheaded by the papacy were sent from Europe to put the Holy Land under Christian control. Crusades had the effect of creating a long-lasting, deep-seated hatred and mistrust between Christians and Muslims. The leaders of the Islamic and Christian countries often prevented each other's merchants from crossing their borders. Corsairs (pirates) on both sides were encouraged to attack ships and pillage cargoes of traders aligned with the other faith. Thanks to the substantial revenue brought to both sides through trade, a neutral party was needed. Radhanite Jews filled that role. The Radhanites had built a network of Jewish traders throughout Europe, Africa, the Middle East, and Asia as far as China. They were mostly tolerated and even welcomed by Arabs and Christians. Arab traders had a long relationship with Radhanites, who were established in cities all across the known world, including the Far East. The Radhanites functioned as go-betweens that kept lines of communication open, as bankers who would honor letters of credit drawn on each other, and above all as trusted business partners.[20] They were also traders who could pass freely across the borders of Islamic and Christian countries.[21] Jews had a virtual monopoly of the European spice trade until the emergence of Italian mercantile city-states such as Genoa, Pisa, Amalfi, and Venice, which saw them as unwelcome competitors.

Venice, ruled by merchants with a keen eye for profits, had cultivated a long trading relationship with the Arabs in Egypt. Their navy and transport ships were numerous and controlled the eastern Mediterranean. This city-state, more than any other in Western Europe, became the entry portal for spices (especially pepper), silks, and exotic goods from the Far East and the Levant. Demand outstripped supply, and despite the Ottoman conquest of Constantinople in 1493 (marking the end of both the Byzantine Empire and the Dark Ages), Venice retained many of its trading privileges and continued to control the flow of pepper into Europe.

Pepper Producers

So far, this chapter has been all about the demand and distribution side of the pepper story. Pepper was a source of great wealth for the Indian producers. From 100 CE until the sixteenth-century European intervention in the Mughal Empire, India was the world's wealthiest country, controlling or producing between one-quarter and one-third of the world's output. Europe, the Middle East, and Southeast Asia paid for indigo, muslin, calico, Kashmir textiles, opium, cinnamon, and pepper with precious metals (gold and silver). The balance of trade at that time heavily favored India, who needed or wanted very little from the west. Precious metals were the primary medium of exchange. Although pepper did not command the highest price, it was the most important because the volume exceeded that of all other exports. The development of trade routes by both sea and land along with a culture of joint family entrepreneurism[22] and industriousness brought great prosperity to the people and rulers of early India.

Although India was located near the limit of the Chinese merchant and military navies, excellent trade relationships developed between the China and the Malabar Coast during the ninth century throughout the medieval period. China had the largest ships in the world at that time,[23] and they played a significant role in transporting pepper germplasm (seeds and cuttings) throughout the Far East. The Chinese purchased seventy-five thousand pounds per year, equivalent to the total quantity imported into Europe during the first half of the tenth century. Government officials and private soldiers in China received part of their salary in pepper by 1425 CE.

In the north of India, incursions by Persians, Greeks, and Romans led to the construction of cities with defensive walls, deepwater harbors, and extensive fortifications. The southern Malabar coast (modern-day Kerala) was not well connected to the north, and thus these foreign invaders did not go there. Roman, Greek, or Persian ruins are not found in southern India. Many of the Malabar Coast cities were not well fortified, and there were few deepwater harbors to accommodate ocean trading vessels. The strong wet monsoon winds and seasonal storm surges from the Arabian Sea had created a series of sandy barrier islands with few deepwater harbors and ports. The Malabar region produced a great deal of high-quality pepper. Cargoes were shipped in shallow draft boats along the placid backwaters[24] to those deepwater ports where larger ships could convey the cargoes to the west. Consequently, the rulers of the Malabar region were relatively independent from each other and small in size. Religious tolerance was widely accepted, and communities of Christians, Muslims, Hindus, Jains, and Jews lived in close proximity without problems, much as they do today in the Indian state of Kerala. Larger cities, such as Kochi (Cochin), Khozikode, and Goa with deepwater harbors were collection points for pepper. Local rulers (called Zamorins) controlled and taxed all pepper transactions and were very wealthy as a result.

Pepper and Colonial Imperialism   3

A T THE END OF THE MEDIEVAL PERIOD, Europe was ready for better times. The fifteenth century brought a great deal of prosperity to northwestern Europe. High wages (even for the lower classes of society), low rents, and low food prices enabled everyone to live better. Even the poor were able to eat meat.[1] Prosperity had the effect of increasing demand for pepper and other luxury goods. For most of the world's history, pepper was not hard to find, but it was expensive to buy. Even today, high-quality specialty pepper can be expensive,[2] although ordinary black pepper is much less costly today than it was at the end of the Dark Ages in 1438. Currency, precious metals, and other exchange media have varied in value dramatically over time, so a comparison based on a laborer's hourly pay to buy a given quality of pepper is better. John Munro (University of Toronto) provides a comparison of prices paid for pepper in terms of an average worker's labor hours. In London in 1483, a master carpenter required two and a quarter days to earn a pound of pepper. Today, a similar job paying $35 dollars per hour needs only fourteen minutes to purchase the same amount of pepper.[3]

Muslim traders, looking for increases in the supply of pepper, introduced the *Piper nigrum* vine to northern Sumatra, where Lampung pepper is produced today. Prices rose, and trading cities like Venice and Genoa became extremely wealthy. Venice had a near-monopoly on the trade in spices that seemed unbreakable.

By end of the fifteenth century, adventurous travelers had visited all of Europe, much of Asia, and parts of Africa without having to cross the vast Atlantic, Indian, and Pacific Oceans. Some travelers originated in Europe, but Chinese, Arab, and North African travelers[4] brought new and unique products with them. Despite rumors of its existence from Viking times, the Americas were largely unknown, with the exception of the Grand Banks where the Irish and Basque had been fishing cod for many years. In the fifteenth century, it was well understood (and accepted) that the world was round and that India (the source of pepper) was overland to the east.

Spain and Portugal

The Iberian kings of Spain and Portugal, having cast off the yoke of Islamic occupation by the Moors were hungry for wealth and power. They were aware that a direct route by sea to India would give them a substantial share of the profits from the pepper trade by eliminating countless intermediaries and breaking the near monopoly of the Italian city-states like Venice and Genoa. They thought the potential profits from such a scheme were enormous. Portuguese Prince Henry the Navigator encouraged the development of naval technology and exploration. Armed with substantial knowledge of ocean navigation by the mid-1400s, the Portuguese were not intimidated to venture offshore. By 1469, they had already been travelling south along the west coast of Africa to the Gulf of Guinea for many years[5] in search of gold, spices, slaves, and other sources of wealth. Guinea pepper, melegueta pepper, and other pungent-tasting spices found there were of little interest to a population that had been completely obsessed with pepper for millennia. Although each of these pepper substitutes had its own merits, none was a significant source of wealth.

In 1487, King John II of Portugal dispatched two Arab-speaking spies, Pero da Covilha and Alfonso de Pavia, to scout the location of the foreign spice markets and trade routes. Posing as Moors, they traveled overland to Egypt, East Africa, and finally India. Their report identified the location of Calicut (modern day Kozhikode on the Malabar coast of India), a major spice-trading city in India. After receiving the report, John II was committed to discovery of a sea route around the tip of Africa and east to India. He must have been thrilled when his Captain Bartolomeu Dias rounded the Cape of Good Hope in 1488, eliminating any remaining doubt that such a route existed.

Despite knowledge of Dias's voyage to the Cape, Christopher Columbus was convinced that the shortest route to India was by sea to the west. Columbus had developed flawed calculations of the earth's circumference, and estimated Japan was twenty-three hundred miles west of the Canary Islands, the last victualing station before setting off across the uncharted Atlantic Ocean. He calculated that a crossing would take less than thirty days, just within the limit of food and water provisions that could be stowed onboard for such a voyage. Armed with his calculations and promises of untold wealth, he shopped around his ideas to King John II of Portugal and the rulers of Genoa, Venice, and England. After consulting with their own experts, each of them denied his request for funding three ships. Finally, Queen Isabella of Aragon and King Ferdinand of Castile agreed to his proposal in the hope that this daring and risky investment would pay off.

Columbus set sail with the now famous *Nina*, *Pinta*, and *Santa Maria* on August 3, 1492. He arrived at the Canary Islands six days later to make some repairs and take on supplies for the voyage into the great unknown. He left the Canary Islands on September 6. Thirty-four days later with supplies running short, he sighted land on October 12, 1492. Columbus was ecstatic. He concluded that his calculations were correct, and his land-fall could be none other than India, somewhere to the south of Japan! He was incredibly lucky. Had the Americas not been in his way, he would have literally sailed into the sunset, never to be seen again.

Returning from his first voyage in 1492, Columbus brought back some gold and pearls (which were of great interest), a few kidnapped natives (a potential source of slaves[6]), turkeys, tobacco, and pineapples (none of which were considered to have much potential as a source of wealth). The economic results of the first voyage were disappointing. He struggled to validate the financing of the trip to the Spanish monarchs. Columbus was able to secure funding for a second voyage in 1493 by writing numerous letters to the Spanish court that overstated the value of his findings. The possibilities of these new, unclaimed lands, its people, and unknown potential wealth must have swayed them to fund another voyage.

Spain and Portugal made a treaty after Dias's and Columbus's first voyages to ensure that their exploration activities and claims to new lands did not lead to conflict with each other. The Treaty of Tordesillas (1494) gave all lands west of a demarcation line halfway between Cape Verdes and His-paniola (newly discovered by Columbus) to Spain and all lands east of the line to Portugal. At the time, latitude was determined with reasonable accuracy using the astrolabe, but the ability to measure longitude was dodgy at best,[7] making it difficult to arbiter the east–west provisions of the treaty. The treaty did not mention the line of demarcation on the other side of the world (somewhere in the Pacific, where east and west would meet), but it did give the Spanish uncontested claims to North, Central, and most of South America (with the exception of the eastern part of Brazil, deemed to be on the Portuguese side). As a result, Spain did not become a major player in the spice trade, preferring to take fortunes in Aztec and Inca gold. The treaty left Portugal with Africa (they were already exploiting the west coast), Brazil, and more importantly India and the yet-to-be discovered Spice Islands farther east.

On Columbus's second voyage in 1495, a knowledgeable natural philosopher, Diego Álvarez Chanca,[8] brought back and documented the first capsicums, believed to be *Capsicum annum* (chili pepper). Columbus brought back allspice, another in a string of poor substitutes for peppercorns, and thus of little commercial value. In Spanish, allspice is *pimiento de Jamaica* (Jamaican pepper). Excited by the prospect of extending their rule and with the support of the Catholic Church (eager to spread Christianity), Columbus completed four voyages and founded the second known settlement in the new world.[9] He visited and named a large number of the islands and coastal areas of the Caribbean basin, including coastal Central America and Venezuela. Until his death in 1506, he firmly believed he had found India, just not the pepper-producing Malabar Coast.

A year after Columbus's return from his second voyage in 1496, Vasco da Gama, financed by Portuguese King Don Manuel (John II's successor), set off with a fleet of four ships and 170 men to complete the discovery of the sea route to India by rounding the Cape of Good Hope and going east. At one point, lacking sufficient funds to resupply his fleet near modern-day Kenya, he resorted to piracy. When da Gama arrived in Calicut, India, his ships were badly in need of repair and resupply. A Jewish trader (part of the network established by the Radhanites) in Calicut extended credit based on da Gama's letters of authorization from King Don Manuel. The bill for these services was sent overland and presented for payment in the Portuguese court long before da Gama returned, thus informing the Portuguese rulers that their expeditionary voyage had arrived in India. Another surprise was in store for the Portuguese. Thomas the Apostle had landed in Kerala and established a community of Christians in 52 CE. The Christians were well received and had been granted many rights and privileges, including exemption from import duties, sales taxes, and slave taxes over the years. Christianity was well established with churches and congregations throughout the Malabar region.

Vasco da Gama did not have much gold or silver for payment and only a small supply of rather paltry gifts to present to the leaders of port cities along the way. Pots, metal goods, and colored cloth had been received by local leaders and traders along the coast of Africa. Not so by the sophisticated and wealthy Zamorins of the Malabar coast. His introductory gifts amused but did not impress the Zamorin of Calicut, who was from a long line of sophisticated rulers who had built relationships with Muslim, Jewish, and Chinese traders. However, despite his apparent arrogance, da Gama managed to obtain two shiploads of pepper for the return journey. Local Arab traders complained to the Zamorin that da Gama did not pay the customary export duties and tried to impede his departure. Da Gama kidnapped several of them as hostages and left Calicut in 1498. It seems that the first contact was off to a rocky start, but the Portuguese had secured the all-important first-mover advantage in the spice-trade race that would follow.

After a harrowing voyage lasting more than a year, two of da Gama's ships returned in 1499 with a cargo of pepper worth approximately sixty times the cost of the expedition, a substantial return for the Portuguese rulers, despite the loss of two ships and over half the men.

Learning from da Gama's experience, Don Manuel commissioned an armada consisting of thirteen well-armed ships and fifteen hundred men four years later. Under the command of Pedro Álvares Cabral,[10] they carried valuable gifts and diplomatic letters to establish or confirm relationships along the way and for the Zamorin of Calicut. It was clear that to make the sea route possible the Portuguese needed to secure agreements for access to ports along the east coast of Africa, vital for the repair and resupply of ships. Cabral's orders were to secure a treaty with the Zamorin of Calicut, establish a factory (trading) house in Calicut, and take a group of Franciscan priests with him to bring Roman Catholicism to the local Christians. The factory house, under the direction of the factor, would purchase quantities of pepper all year long in order to avoid the temporary shortages and price spikes when a Portuguese ship arrived seeking a large cargo of pepper.

Cabral's voyage was a diplomatic disaster. After he secured a treaty granting him trading rights and a factory house in Calicut, local Arab merchants (the memory of their last interaction with the Portuguese still fresh in their minds) rioted, killing the newly appointed factor and more than fifty Portuguese sailors that were on shore leave. The Zamorin did nothing about it, so Cabral took matters into his own hands. He attacked ten Arab merchant ships in the harbor, killed their crews, seized their cargoes, and burned the ships. Then he bombarded Calicut to a heap of smoldering ruins with his ships' cannons, starting a war with Calicut that would last for the next ten years. Having quite literally burned his bridges, Cabral headed south to Kochi (modern-day Cochin). The Zamorins of Kochi were quite pleased with the destruction of their rivals in Calicut and granted Cabral a treaty to trade pepper and the right to build and maintain a factory house.

Photo 3.1.   Burial site of Vasco de Gama, December 24, 1524, St. Francis Church, Cochin.
J. Barth (Author)

Cabral purchased some pepper (his holds already full of pepper pillaged from the Arab merchant ships) and set off just in time to avoid an armada of eighty vessels sent by the Zamorin of Calicut to take revenge.

After Columbus and Vasco da Gama, it did not take long before large numbers of voyages of colonization and exploitation to the New World were undertaken. The rush for riches and territory by the seafaring nations of Europe had begun. The once sleepy coastal town of San Lucar de Barrameda became the Cape Canaveral of the day, the principal launching points for ships heading to unknown lands in Africa and North and South America searching for wealth and territory. Spain financed Magellan's expedition to continue the search for a sea route to the west, resulting in the first circumnavigation of the Earth in 1522. The Portuguese learned that cities along the Malabar coast had no fortifications in place to defend against an attack from the sea and that local trading vessels were equally vulnerable. The Portuguese mission switched from trading for pepper to taking whatever they wanted by force of arms. In all, thirteen Portuguese armadas were dispatched to the Far East over a period of fourteen years.

The heavily armed ships dominated the seas and blockaded the transport of pepper by all other ships unless permits had been purchased from the Portuguese authorities in the area. Marines enforced Portuguese control on land. They taxed the local traders under threat of expulsion and built fortifications to guard against other European powers. For a time, the Portuguese effectively created their own monopoly on trade in the Indian Ocean. To manage the Portuguese interests at the edge of the known world, the Portuguese created the Estado da India (Portuguese State of India) in 1505, only a few years after Cabral's voyage. The Estado da India was governed from Kochi, by a viceroy,[11] Francisco de Almeida. The viceroy was responsible for all the diplomatic, military, and commercial interests in the area. Not satisfied with the Malabar Coast, Portuguese ships ventured farther. In the same year, they took control of Sri Lanka for its cinnamon, and in 1511 they crossed the Bay of Bengal to the Straits of Malacca. The Straits of Malacca separate the island of Sumatra from the Malay Peninsula, the only passage linking the Indian Ocean with the South China Sea. Without access to straits like Malacca, ships could sail for weeks or months without encountering another vessel. In 1522, the Portuguese conquered the wealthy port city of Malacca, the choke point for shipments of cloves, nutmeg, and mace from the Indonesian Spice Islands (Malucu Islands) located two thousand miles farther east.

In Venice, the cost of pepper (and spices in general) increased due to the shortages caused by the Portuguese blockade of sea-going Arab traders. Furthermore, Portuguese ships would arrive in Mediterranean ports loaded with large amounts of pepper for sale at lower prices. The Jesuit priests who accompanied the Portuguese established themselves in communities and played a role in introducing the pepper plant to many other areas in the equatorial zone (including Brazil). Once unique to India, pepper now grows in many tropical areas, separated by thousands of miles of ocean. In addition, the priests were able to convert a substantial number of local inhabitants to Roman Catholicism due to the long-standing spirit of religious tolerance in Asia. (European-style Catholic churches and cathedrals built in the fifteenth and sixteenth centuries are now popular tourist attractions in Malabar Coast cities today.) For a time, the Portuguese had it all. But nothing lasts forever.

The British and Dutch

The British were slow to enter the spice race in the Far East. England had a long-standing alliance with Portugal (the Anglo-Portuguese Alliance of 1373) against their mutual archenemy, Spain, and did not want to encroach on their ally's imperial ambitions. The British were content to trade for pepper arriving in the Levant overland by caravan. Canny British merchants were also skeptical about the financial success of the Portuguese voyages. They were waiting to see how many of the Portuguese ships returned from the long voyage to India and how much cargo they carried before making any decisions about investing in voyages of their own. Opportunities for England to join in the spice trade were about to open up.

A suspension of the Anglo-Portuguese Alliance took place in 1580 when Portugal joined with Spain (the so-called Iberian Union) in order to declare war against the Dutch. The Dutch were a rival seafaring nation, eager to make their fortunes in the spice trade. The British secured help from the Dutch to defeat the Spanish Armada sent to invade England in 1588. Letters of marque authorized privately owned ships (privateers) to take, pillage, and burn ships of the enemy for profit. British privateers (most famously Sir Francis Drake) had been actively attacking Spanish treasure ships loaded with gold and silver. When the British fleet captured the heavily laden Portuguese ship *Madre de Deus* off the Azores in 1592, they were astonished to find cargo from India on board worth 500,000 pounds (including 425 tons of pepper), half the value of the English treasury at the time. The news of such wealth electrified seafaring European countries interested in grabbing a share of the wealth.

Portuguese ships and trading posts became fair game for Dutch and British ships seeking a share of the lucrative spice trade. The Dutch sent Cornelis de Houteman to find the sources of the Portuguese cargo. In 1594, Houteman sailed through the Sunda Straits (between Sumatra and Java) to Banten. The Portuguese did not patrol the Sunda Straits at this time, enabling Houteman to enter the area uncontested. Although it was a disastrous voyage, both financially and physically (only eighty-seven out of a crew of 249 returned), it opened the way for more than sixty-five Dutch voyages in the next five years. At this time, the British merchants noticed that the Dutch were buying every ship they could get their hands on, which piqued their interest in the spice trade by sea.

After the Treaty of London (1604) ended the war between Spain and England, the British turned their sights to the Americas to realize their colonial ambitions. They established thirteen colonies in what is now the United States, as well as Newfoundland, parts of southern Ontario (Upper Canada), and several islands in the Caribbean. Cod from the Grand Banks, sugar from the Caribbean, cotton and tobacco from the southern colonies, and furs from northern Canada were very lucrative. The British also became slave traders, slaves being essential to the production of sugar, cotton, and tobacco.

The first incursion into the Portuguese trading empire occurred in 1605, when Dutch merchant Captain Steven Vanderhagen clashed with Portuguese on the west and north coasts of Java. Ill-treatment of the locals by the Portuguese had evolved into a deep-seated hatred, and the Dutch had no difficulty allying themselves with an anti-Portuguese Muslim leader on Ambon Island (Indonesia), the site of a Portuguese fort. After taking the fort, the Dutch were granted the authority to trade in pepper, and they set up their first base of operations in the Far East. From there, they set up factory houses in Aceh at the north end of Sumatra, where pepper plants had been introduced by Arab and Indian traders many years before.

The common practice for mercantile investment in the spice trade had been to create a company for each voyage. Investors would buy shares, and the capital was used to buy a ship, hire a crew, load it with supplies, and send it off to trade for pepper. At the conclusion of the voyage, the cargo was sold, the crew paid off, and the ship put up for sale. Profits were distributed to the shareholders, and the company was dissolved. These investments were very risky. At worst, ships and their cargoes were lost at sea resulting in a total loss. A coffee shop owned by Edward Lloyd on Tower Street in London evolved into the first marine insurance company (Lloyds of London) providing shipping companies with a hedge against the loss of their ships. A more common problem was that many ships arrived within a similar time (due to the seasonality of trade winds) and prices would drop suddenly with a glut of newly landed pepper. Being among the first ships to arrive meant that you could get higher prices for your cargo, and the profits increased for owners of fast ships. Those arriving even a few days later obtained much lower prices for their hard-won cargoes. Ever larger and faster ships were built to support the spice trade. It made good business sense to form cartels to spread the risk over multiple ships and to manage the orderly release of spice cargoes, thereby stabilizing prices. The governments of the day wanted a share of the proceeds, but had little desire to manage the risk or finance the military support necessary for the spice trade. The solution was to privatize their imperial ambitions.

The East India companies served such a purpose. After the British had taken the *Madre de Deus*, Austria, Denmark, France, England, the Netherlands, and Sweden created "East India Companies" to develop and oversee their national interest in the spice trade. These organizations had quasi-governmental powers including the waging of war, imprisonment and execution of convicts, negotiation of treaties, creation of their own currency, and establishment of colonies.[12] The power of some of these companies was immense: the British East India Company had a private army of two hundred sixty thousand soldiers in 1803, twice the size of the British armed forces at the time.

With its roots as the Pepperer's Guild in London (1180), the British East India Company received a royal charter from Queen Elizabeth I in 1600. It has been suggested that the motivation to found the East India Company was a rise in the price of pepper from 18 to 23 shillings per pound being charged by the Dutch, who supplied much of England's pepper at that time. In a decrepit building on Leaden Hall Street in London, a group of 125 merchants capitalized the "Governor and Company of Merchants of London Trading into the East Indies" (soon after to be known as the British East India Company) with an initial layout of 72,000 pounds.[13] With the approval of Queen Elizabeth I, the company received a charter granting them exclusive trading rights east of the Cape of Good Hope and west of the Straits of Magellan. At one time, the British East India Company was in control of half the world's trade with the Far East and largely responsible for the creation and administration of the British Empire. The Dutch East India Company (also known as the Verenigde Oostindische Compagnie, or VOC) was a similar body, created in 1602.

Shortly after receiving their charter, the VOC established their headquarters on Ambon Island in 1602 and opened commercial bases in Batavia (now Jakarta) in 1611. The Dutch relentlessly drove the Portuguese out of many of their bases over the next fifty years. Sometimes they did it on their own, sometimes in alliance with local leaders.[14] With the suspension of the Anglo-Portuguese alliance, English ships also took action against strategically important Portuguese holdings north of modern-day Mumbai (Surat, 1614) and the Straits of Ormuz (1622) on the Persian Gulf.

Power and Piracy

From a financial perspective, the Portuguese spice monopoly in the 1600s was not as profitable as it appeared to be.[15] Most Portuguese ships were designed for exploration and fighting and had crews of more than one hundred men. They did not have massive cargo capacity, since a substantial amount of the space below decks was needed for crew accommodation, food, water, and weaponry. The passage by sea was seasonal and took a long time. Ships were often lost, and the costs of repairs, crews, and supplies was great. Internal theft due to poor control over ships' supplies bled away a huge proportion of the revenues from the transport and sale of pepper. The cost of military control of the Malabar Coast, Indian Ocean, Bay of Bengal, and the Malacca Straits also figured into every pound of pepper.

Pepper prices were coming down due to the large increase in supply, and comparatively lower overland transport costs. Slow (or no) replacement of lost ships and shortages of crews saw a gradual reduction in Portugal's power in the region. The Portuguese fleet, once several hundred ships strong, was outnumbered and outgunned by more than eighty enemy galleons operating in the region.

Beginning in 1626, Lisbon began sending annual cash subsidies to the Estado da India (the Portuguese equivalent of an East India company), something they could ill afford to do given problems defending their homeland and Brazil.[16] The first Anglo-Dutch War (1652–1654) established England as the dominant sea power in the world but did not change the Netherland's increasing domination of the spice trade. The Portuguese, caught between economic losses of the Estado da India and the inability to enforce their hold on trade, had no choice but to sign peace agreements with the British and Dutch East India companies (1663), granting the victors trade and administrative rights to most of the Portuguese holdings in India.

The Danish, Austrians, Swedes, and Prussians tried but failed to get a piece of the action in India. In 1664, French finance minister Jean-Baptiste Colbert launched the French equivalent of the English East India Company. The French were able to seize control of a few cities, including Pondicherry (east coast, north of Chennai) and Chandernagore (near modern-day Kolkata); however, their trade volume was only half of the British East India Company's take. The French and English were often at war with each other in various parts of the world. India was no exception. Near the end of the Seven Years' War (1756–1763), the French surrendered and lost all their holdings in India.

A second war between the Dutch and English (1665–1667) damaged the Dutch ability to control trade; however both sides suffered significant losses and had to rebuild their fleets. The vice-regal Dutch and British East India Companies engaged in multiple naval battles over the next twenty-two years. However, through it all, the Dutch VOC remained the dominant force in the region. The English focused a great deal of their efforts on India, China, and Japan because the Dutch retained control of the East Indies (modern-day Indonesia). The British East India Company traded cotton and opium from India to the Chinese and Indonesians for tea, silk, and spices that were shipped back to England or its colonies.

During the time of the Dutch domination of the spice trade, the Dutch governor of Malabar, Hendrick Van Rheede, produced a major work cataloging the plants found in the Western Ghats that was published in 1678–1693. It consisted of twelve volumes written in Latin, each about two hundred pages in length, with contributions by European and South Asian experts.

Elihu Yale is the first person born in America to be significantly involved in the pepper trade. Yale was an Englishman who was born in Boston in 1649 to Welsh parents, who moved back to England when he was three years old. Yale was a controversial figure. He worked for the British East India Company as the president of the Fort George settlement (modern-day Chennai, formerly known as Madras) beginning in 1684 for almost twenty years. He became very wealthy by arranging secret contracts with local merchants and was involved in shipping slaves (including children) back to England,[17] where some entered domestic service. Charges of corruption were brought against him near the end of his tenure with the British East India Company, but they were eventually dropped. Shady arrangements and corrupt practices were common among the British, VOC, and Estado da India administrators. Despite the dubious source of his wealth, Yale supported the Collegiate School of the Colony of Connecticut with a significant donation. In 1718, three years before his death, it was renamed Yale College (modern Yale University) in his honor.

In 1776, no longer being subjects of the British Crown, Americans were free to try their luck in the Far East. The first American citizen to enter the spice trade in a significant way was Captain Jonathan Carnes of the *Rajah*. The *Rajah* was a new, American-built, lightly armed schooner. It was manned by a crew of only ten seamen and had a substantial cargo capacity. American schooners were designed to fish for cod on the Grand Banks of Newfoundland and other Atlantic coastal waters to bring the fresh fish to port rapidly without the need for salting. The *Rajah* could sail closer to the wind and easily outrun much larger, heavily armed ships. Given the name of the vessel, one could argue that the *Rajah* was purpose-built for a shot at the spice trade. Carnes (who was also an American privateer) managed to purchase a shipload of pepper direct from natives in Sumatra. The *Rajah*'s cargo of 158,544 pounds of pepper landed in its home port of Salem, Massachusetts, on October 15, 1799. This amount of pepper was far in excess of demand from the American states; however, canny Salem merchants eagerly purchased all the pepper at the full price demanded. Most of the pepper was exported to England and British colonies as far away as Australia and New Zealand.[18] Carnes kept the details of his voyage secret and completed a second voyage (1801) before other Salem sea captains found the source. In the following years, several larger American ships brought back huge cargoes of pepper for the international market.[19] Salem became the most important pepper-trading center in the world for the next forty years.[20] The decline of the American pepper trade was in part due to the outbreak of the Civil War in 1861.

The Dutch and British East India Companies' vice-regal powers began to wane toward the end of the eighteenth century. Dutch power declined massively by the conclusion of the fourth Anglo–Dutch war in 1784. Heavy losses left the Netherlands vulnerable to French ground troops in the Napoleonic wars, and the Netherlands became a client (occupied) state of France (the Batavian Republic) in 1795. After the Dutch nationalized the VOC in 1796, the British soundly defeated the Dutch navy in the Battle of Camperdown (1797). The remnants of the once mighty VOC were dissolved on December 31, 1799. England took over most of the Dutch colonies by the conclusion of the Napoleonic wars (1815) with the exception of the Dutch East Indies (modern-day Indonesia), the Dutch Antilles,[21] Surinam on the north coast of South America, and a trading post in Japan.

The British East India Company began to lose its vice-regal power in the region with the passage of the East India Act of 1774, which transferred the rule of India to the crown. Lord Cornwallis, appointed governor general of India in 1786, laid the foundations of British rule. The British East India Company's monopoly on trade in India was withdrawn in 1813; however, it continued to possess the monopoly on trade with China. The Indian Rebellion of 1857 that had devastated large parts of the country was widely blamed on the British East India Company. In the following year, Parliament passed the Government of India Act and the British East India Company was nationalized. The Crown took over its land holdings and all remaining administrative and military control. After years of declining financial performance, the British East India Company was dissolved in 1874, making it legal for all British citizens to engage in trade with India. Queen Victoria became the Empress of India in 1876. The wooden sailing ships were gradually replaced by steam-powered, steel-hulled vessels, increasing both the reliability and speed of international shipping. The state-controlled trading monopolies were finished. It was much more efficient for countries to collect import duties and taxes from private spice-trading companies than to manage the trade themselves.

Many spice traders entered the business on both sides of the Atlantic, one of the most notable being the McCormick Company founded in 1889 by Willoughby McCormick in Baltimore. Beginning as a family-owned spice trading business, McCormick is the largest spice merchant in the world. They operate from fifty facilities located in twenty-six countries. McCormick, a Fortune 1000 company, has well over $4 billion in annual sales and is publicly traded on the New York Stock Exchange.

Pepper Economics **4**

IN 2017, THE PRICE OF PEPPER had fallen to $4,130 US per ton from $10,908 US in 2015. The world demand for pepper reached a new high of 446,000 tons, trending steadily higher, but production had also grown to a staggering 523,000 tons.[1] Inventories of unsold pepper were sure to grow over the next three years. Some analysts predict that a full year's supply of pepper will be held in inventories around the world by 2020. For pepper farmers, the future does not look bright. Although the value of pepper traded in the world is nothing to sneeze at (approximately $4.5 billion US annually in 2015), it is significantly less than other crops produced in similar geographical and climatic regions. Coffee ($189 billion), natural rubber ($21.8 billion), tea ($13.2 billion), and cocoa ($8.2 billion) have a much larger economic impact on third world trade and the livelihood of the working poor.

This chapter is not about the statistics of the 2017 pepper situation, although they are crucially important to the people involved in the pepper trade. It is about the factors that affect the pepper trade and the people who bring it to our tables. Many readers have a rudimentary knowledge of economics. The basics are simple: a downward sloping demand curve reveals that as the price goes lower, people will buy more. An upward sloping supply curve says that if the price is higher, more growers will enter the markets and increase the amount produced. Economists teach us that if we superimpose these two curves, there is an equilibrium price and quantity defined by the intersection of the supply and demand curves. No doubt this is true; however, there are many complexities in the marketplace that make this simple intuitive relationship less useful than one might think. In a highly fragmented industry with many small producers located in more than a dozen countries, the economics of pepper takes on an entirely different perspective.

The demand for pepper is segmented: it is used in the home; for commercial food processing; and for cosmetic, pharmaceutical, and insecticidal purposes. Other ways to segment pepper are by type (green, black, white, and red peppercorns), production region (India, Brazil, Indonesia, Malaysia, to name just a few), and the form in which it is used (pepper that is ground or whole, processed, and extracts such as oleoresins and piperine).

The price and quantity of pepper purchased are affected by many things. Not every user wants the same quality of pepper. Manufacturers of peppermills that fill their grinders as a marketing tool will buy old, cheaper pepper to minimize their costs. Companies selling ground pepper or spice blends are unlikely to buy top-quality pepper. On the other hand, gourmet food stores seek a variety of top-quality peppercorns from different countries to tantalize their shoppers. Producers of oleoresins and essential oils have their own requirements that trade off the cost of the pepper they buy against the price they receive for their products. Government regulations defining contamination with extraneous matter, chemical residues, bacteria, and viruses vary across different importing countries, and they change over time. Different farming methods produce widely varying yields and corresponding differences in price and quality. The point is that pepper is not a single commodity, even though all of its production comes from the *Piper nigrum* plant.

Table 4.1.   Kinds of *Piper nigrum* Products

Green Pepper:
- Bulk, canned or bottled in brine
- Pickled in vinegar and oil
- Green pepper paste
- Cured green pepper
- Frozen fresh
- Sun dried, dehydrated, or freeze dried

Black, White, and Red Pepper
- Peppercorns
- Ground
(black* and white only)

Pepper Extracts
- Oleoresin
- Essential oil
- Piperine

* 48% of the total.

Pepper Demand

World demand for pepper has increased steadily. Growth is best measured over longer time periods using a statistic called compound average growth rates (CAGR). CAGR is used instead of simple growth rate because the measurement of pepper demand is constantly changing, increasing and decreasing over the various times when it is reported during the course of multiple years. CAGR "smoothes" out the bumps and lumps to provide an overall indication of market growth, including growth that occurs between the times when reports are received. The CAGR over the past twenty-eight years is 2.47 percent annually, almost identical to CAGR over the past five years.

Analysts have divided the world demand for pepper into regions that are importers of pepper and regions that produce pepper. Importing Asian markets include Japan, New Zealand, and Australia, but not China, Malaysia, and Indonesia. It is important to keep in mind that countries that produce pepper are also significant users of pepper. India is a very good example.

India has a huge domestic demand for pepper. It remains one of the world's largest consumers of the commodity, with domestic consumption estimated at sixty-two thousand tons a year. India is producing just enough pepper to meet its own internal demand, suggesting that it neither imports

Table 4.2.   World Pepper Demand by Region (2017)

Region	Tons (Thousands)	CAGR (5yr)
Importing Regions		
Europe	85	1.8%
The Americas	69	2.1%
Middle East	40	3.4%
Africa	32	3.2%
Asia Region	25	2.9%
Others	22	1.2%
Total	273	2.3%
Producing Regions		
India	62	1.9%
China	53	3.7%
Indonesia	11	2.0%
Malaysia	9	2.0%
Others	39	2.7%
Total	173	2.3%
World Consumption	446	2.4%

Source: A. Van Gulik, Nedspice Pepper Report, ESA Conference, Bordeaux, France, 2017.

nor exports pepper. This is not true: a substantial amount of India's pepper is exported due it its superior quality (and somewhat higher price). Lower-cost imported pepper from Sri Lanka and Vietnam supply a significant proportion of India's domestic demand. Kerala manufactures most of the world's pepper extracts (oleoresins and piperine); consequently, India imports a substantial amount of lower-cost pepper from Vietnam and Sri Lanka for this purpose. The importation of lower-cost pepper concerns local growers, due to downward price pressures as well as the possibility that some traders may substitute imported pepper for Indian-grown pepper.[2]

Historically, the demand for pepper in both importing and producing economies has increased at nearly the same compound average growth rate (CAGR) of 2.3 percent. The importing economies use nearly 40 percent of all the pepper produced, India and China together using 25 percent of all the pepper in the world. The demand for pepper from Asian markets and China alone has increased 400 percent from 1991 to 2011. Growth of the demand for pepper is highest in the Middle East, followed by China and Africa. Together, the population of these regions is three billion people. Even small increases in individual pepper use will have a substantial impact on the world demand for pepper. Looking to the future, Persistent Market Research, a company based in New York, predicts a CAGR of 6.1 percent through 2024.[3] European and American demand growth is lower; however, they remain the largest importers of pepper in the world. In short, emerging economies will most likely have the greatest effect on pepper demand in the future.

The major factor driving pepper market growth is its use as a flavoring ingredient in food. Spice industry experts know that consumers increasingly want big, bold flavors for a more intense taste experience.[4] Spices are a cost-effective way to change the style and taste of common, locally produced foods into exotic dishes across cultural lines. Individual consumption of pepper in the home (particularly in the large populations of emerging economies) is one reason demand is on the rise. Demand from commercial food processing is another reason. Food processing in Israel alone is a $15.9 billion industry. This is attributable to changes in food purchase and consumption behavior. A growing trend in the world is that people are eating a larger proportion of foods prepared outside the home. By some estimates, Canadians will spend almost 30 percent of their food budget in meals prepared in foodservice facilities.[5] In the past, restaurants and takeouts have been the main benefactors of this shift away from meals prepared in the home. A fast-growing entrant into this market is the "grocerant," a combination of a restaurant and grocery store, where people can purchase a ready-to-eat meal to eat on-site or to take home along with grocery items that will be used to prepare food in the home. Grocerant stores are designed with their ready-to-eat meals displayed at the front of the store for easier, quicker access by hungry, time-pressured customers.

Grocery stores that have competed on price for many years are discovering the higher profit margins and almost infinite varieties of ready-to-eat foods. As stated in the 2018 Canada's Food Price Report,[6] convenience trumps price. Consumers are seeking solutions that enable them to maximize their free time. A 2006 study of UK consumers revealed nearly 60 percent of British consumers spent thirty minutes or less per day preparing meals.[7] Convenience seekers want more than time saving: it also means choice, simplicity, and being healthy. The desire for convenience spans all ages. Senior citizens want smaller package sizes and simple preparation. Stressed-out mid-lifers are trying to achieve a better work-life balance, with healthy, sustainable sources of protein, fats, and carbohydrates. Younger people are experimenting with slow cookers and other preparation technologies that limit the number of dishes, pots, and pans. A broad selection of items reflecting different cuisines in the home pantry provides consumers with the convenience of choice and variety. Above all, convenience products have to taste good. It is no longer necessary to master cooking skills to enjoy a great meal prepared at home.

Convenience food products use spices extensively to enhance the consumer's enjoyment of the food. The grocery basket reflects these changes. The proportion of heat-and-serve items, spice mixes, and so-called "meal kits" is getting larger. Companies like Kraft, Unilever, SunFresh, and a host of smaller food processors are expanding their convenience food product lines to encompass fully prepared and partially prepared meals as well as ingredient kits.[8] Meal kits are rapidly growing in popularity. Meal kits consist of packages with a complete set of ingredients that can be purchased at a store or delivered directly to the home. In Canada, meal kit vendors currently enjoy $120 million in revenues, and their future looks bright.[9] Other processed food segments boosting the demand for pepper are ready-to-eat bakery items, confectionery, sauces, and dressings; prepared meat and poultry products; and bagged snacks.

Spice companies are developing new ways to market pepper. Peppercorns are sold in spice-rack packaging that includes a built-in, disposable grinding mechanism to improve the quality of the pepper in use.

There is a trend toward using increased amounts of spices in food for health reasons. Increasingly, people are looking toward traditional and natural treatments to improve their health. Influential media personalities recommend the health properties of turmeric, cinnamon, pepper, and many other spices on daytime talk shows. A myriad of researchers publish reports citing the health and diet benefits of spices. Consumers are using more pepper because it eases digestion and improves the uptake of nutrients by increasing hydrochloric acid production. Pepper is known to have antioxidant and antibacterial properties.

Manufacturers of cosmetic, pharmaceutical, and nutraceutical products are focusing on new product innovations that use pepper essential oils and extracts. Piperine (the active agent in pepper) increases the absorption of other pharmacological ingredients given orally. Piperine is often included in skin-care product formulations. Applied directly to the skin, it is effective for treating nerve pain (neuralgia) and scabies. It is also an important component of insect repellants. It seems that everywhere you look demand for pepper is increasing.

Pepper Supply

The demand for pepper has been increasing steadily for many years. The supply of pepper varies more than the demand, and thus is an increasingly important factor in price. The pepper supply consists of two parts: pepper production (harvests) and pepper stocks available for sale. Pepper harvests occur at different times in different regions; however, like many agricultural products, harvests are seasonal by nature and companies in the pepper trade must keep stocks of pepper to supply their customers throughout the year.

As seen from the preceding tables, the 2017 production of pepper is outpacing the demand by seventy-seven thousand tons per year. Several countries have increased production recently and are having a major impact on the world supply of pepper. Chief among these is Vietnam, whose

Table 4.3.   Pepper Production March 24

Country	Production in Thousands of Metric Tons (KMT)	%	CAGR (2011–2017)
Vietnam	209	40%	8%
Indonesia	68	13%	1%
India	63	12%	5%
Brazil	63	12%	11%
China	36	7%	2.2%
Cambodia	21	4%	31%
All others	63	12%	0.3%
Total pepper production	523	100%	5.51%

production has doubled from 2007 to 2017, and is supplying 40 percent of the world's demand. New plantings in Vietnam are increasing by 16 percent per year, and recent figures are even higher, suggesting that Vietnam will continue to expand its production for the near future. Most of the Vietnamese pepper farms are along the border regions with Cambodia. It should not be surprising that Cambodia also has increased production and now is the sixth-largest producer in the world, gaining rapidly on fifth-place China. Production in the rest of the world is nearly constant, with only a slight decline over the past five years.

The supply of pepper, regardless of any economic analysis, is the aggregate outcome of decisions made by hundreds of thousands of individual farmers who rely on pepper for their livelihood. There are some exceptions. Amalgamated Plantations PVT, part of the Indian industrial giant TATA, has opened a 245-hectare pepper plantation in the northeast of India. It features high-yield production managed by expert agronomists and world-class processing equipment that provide buyers in Europe and North America with the quality they are looking for. Large corporate producers are few and far between at this time; however, in the future they may industrialize the pepper production industry similar to what happened with coffee production.

The average size of a pepper farm remains less than 0.4 hectares. A farmer who owns or rents a few thousand square meters (less than an acre) of suitable land makes a complex decision whether to plant pepper, an alternate crop, or at its most fundamental level, food to feed his family. Sometimes landowners can choose to dig up their land and extract minerals (tin mining in Muntok is a problem), rendering it useless for any agricultural production in the future. The complexity of the decision depends on several factors, not the least of which is what crop he chooses to plant and how he will grow it.

The same geographic areas that are suitable for growing pepper can also produce natural rubber, coffee, cocoa, tea, and a large variety of other spices. Newly planted cuttings of pepper, coffee, tea, and cocoa take about the same time (three to five years) to yield a commercially viable harvest. Rubber takes five to eight years. Unlike many food crops, changing the crop is a long-term decision that has economic effects lasting twenty years or more (the average productive life of the plant). An analysis by Nedspice managing director Alfons van Gulick[10] suggests that at 2017 prices and costs, pepper remains the best option with a money multiple of 4.4 times the cost of production in year six.[11] This compares favorably to a much lower multiplier of 1.3 for coffee and 0.5 for rubber. The report concludes that pepper remains the farmer's best alternative in a tough situation, at least for the time being.

The yield of the *Piper nigrum* plant varies greatly by how it is cultivated. Intensive, high-yield farming involves substantive input costs such as fertilizers, pesticides, and in some cases the armatures (posts) on which the plant grows. Less intensive farming often has lower yields, but an organically grown crop (with little or no agricultural chemicals used) may fetch a significantly higher price. For example, In India, lower-yield, organic farming practices produce higher-quality Malabar and Tellicherry peppercorns.

Shifting cultivation (known as *jhuming* in India[12]) is a destructive system of land use practiced in many tropical countries. As soils are depleted and crop yields diminish, improved methods of agricultural production (such as fertilizers, pesticides, and replacement plantings of old vines) are foregone in favor of new plantings (slash and burn) or crop changes. Vietnam has been criticized by environmentalists for destroying rainforest jungles to grow intensively farmed mono-crop pepper in full sunlight. Many Indian farmers and officials believe the production of pepper in Karnataka (located in the Western Ghats, east of Goa) is set to overtake production in Kerala its neighbor to the south very soon. The reasons for better production are similar in both Vietnam and Karnataka: pepper is being grown as a mono crop in fresh soil.

The Kerala farmers grow pepper in an ecologically superior, multi-crop cultivation strategy that uses a minimum of fertilizers and pesticides. Multi-crop cultivation includes crops such as coffee that shade the pepper vines, resulting in low yields of higher-quality pepper. Multiple crops with different needs grown on the same land deplete naturally occurring nutrients more slowly. Just across the state line in Karnataka, new pepper plantings are flourishing. Pepper is being planted in fresh, newly cleared land, rich in nutrients and free from soil-borne disease.

Other challenges faced by Kerala pepper farmers are increasing labor costs. State-funded education provides young people in traditional pepper-growing areas such as Idukki with opportunities to work for higher pay in big cities. Aging pepper farmers are choosing to plant cardamom, which brings less revenue per hectare but is less labor intensive to tend and harvest. Similarly, intensively farmed mono-crop pepper produced by comparatively late entrants such as Vietnam, Brazil, Indonesia, and Sri Lanka is giving strong competition to Indian pepper on the world stage. The high price of Indian pepper is what gives farmers in Idukki and Wayanad some consolation in an otherwise bleak background of inefficient production.

Sarawak in Indonesia has one of the highest pepper crop yields in the world due to intensive cultivation and high-density plantings. Let's have a look at the income potential of a typical pepper farm. Smaller holdings are called pepper gardens. The average Sarawak pepper garden is only 2,177 square meters (about half an acre). What does this mean for the farmer? The average planting density is two thousand vines per hectare, each of which can produce three kilograms of pepper: a production rate of six thousand kilograms per hectare. Using a grower's price of $2,600 US per ton in 2017,[13] the average farmer's gross earnings are $3,296. A few years ago (2015), the same farmer was earning twice that much.

Why doesn't the grower receive the full price? The price the grower receives depends on how the crop is sold. Village traders control much of the local market where pepper is grown. Village traders play a number of roles. They aggregate small lots of pepper into the larger quantities that wholesalers buy. The village traders may also act as financiers, offering pre-harvest contracts at discounted prices along with interest-bearing advances to cash-strapped growers.

The village traders ship aggregated loads of pepper to commissioned brokers, who negotiate prices on behalf of corporate spice merchants looking to buy pepper. On any given day, farmers could get higher prices by dealing with a wholesale trader or commissioned broker in a large port city. The main problems for the grower in dealing with a wholesale broker are transportation and the limited quantity of pepper he has available to sell. Wholesale brokers deal in tons, not a few sacks of pepper.

In the past decade, banks and universal access to information are making life more difficult for the village traders and commissioned brokers. Even the smallest farmer has a smartphone and is aware of the market prices published by commodity exchanges within seconds of each transaction. Armed with knowledge of recent prices, his bargaining position with the village trader is vastly improved. Banks specializing in the financing of agricultural enterprises offer competitive interest rates and often are willing to advance 80–90 percent of the crop's value.

Nowhere are the effects of this change in the supply chain more evident than in Idukki, a major producing region in Kerala's Western Ghats area. Village traders, who used to stay open well past midnight as trucks were loaded, close up by six in the evening. Small traders used to assemble up to two tons of pepper daily during January and February, the major harvesting months. Now, cold, cement floors lie empty, with only modest mounds of pepper dumped in corners.

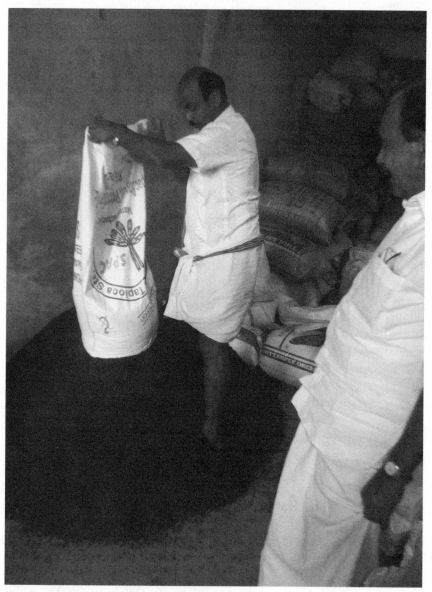

Photo 4.1.   The local village aggregator receives pepper. J. Barth (Author)

The only consolation is that older farmers, having enjoyed long-term relationships with their local trader, are reticent to engage in other, more profitable ways to sell their crop.

The commissioned brokers located in Jew Town, a historic mercantile area of Kochi, who used to finance the chain of pepper traders, have all but disappeared or have altered their business models. Their activity now is restricted mostly to the ginger trade. Out of nearly seventy spice export firms twenty years ago, only a handful are still functioning to date.

India initiated pepper futures over one hundred years ago to provide a mechanism that could safeguard against the price risk of spices handled by traders. The Indian Pepper and Spice Trade Association (IPSTA), also located in Jew Town, took the leading role in establishing future contracts. They had an instrumental effect in stabilizing the market for both producers and consumers. Until 2008, pepper futures from all over the world were transacted on the trading floor located on the second story of the unassuming IPSTA building near the Kochi waterfront.

All IPSTA trading activity ceased in 2016, and the exchange has voluntarily dissolved. The IPSTA building and huge waterfront warehouses, where pepper arriving in boats and barges used to be unloaded

Photo 4.2.   India Pepper and Spice Trade Association Building. J. Barth (Author)

Photo 4.3.   The Pepper Exchange, defunct since 2016. J. Barth (Author)

and stored, have been repurposed as retail stores selling antiques and handicrafts to tourists.

Today, trading of pepper futures is accomplished using computers over the internet. Several exchanges such as Multi Commodity Exchange (MCE) and the National Commodity and Derivatives Exchange (NCDEX) in Mumbai deal in many commodities, including different grades of pepper. Traders and former IPSTA stakeholders in Kerala, many miles away from Mumbai, have expressed apprehension about the new exchanges because they fear market manipulation by cartels, unreliable delivery of product, and inaccurate product grading. In the old days, pepper was graded in the Jew Town warehouses adjacent to the IPSTA building. Relationships between growers, village traders, and brokers were personal and based on trust. Anyone can become a trader through one of a large commodity exchanges located in Mumbai fifteen hundred kilometers to the north. MCE and NCDEX started trading small pepper contracts of one quintal (100 kg) to encourage participation by small traders and speculators.

Future contracts are an important component of commodity markets. Future markets are standardized as to trading specifications (size of the commodity and quality) and terms of delivery (place and date). Futures contracts transfer risk from hedgers (risk avoiders) to speculators (risk takers). Spice traders purchase future contracts to hedge against price and supply variations. For example, in the absence of information about next year's harvest and price, a hedger would buy pepper future contracts for delivery next year and lock in their costs. Speculators buy and sell future contracts in the hope that prices will rise and they can sell the contract for a profit. A speculator would seldom take delivery of a pepper shipment.

Market manipulation through commodity exchanges can take place. Powerful individuals or organizations have attempted to "corner" the market. This can happen when a large buyer acquires substantial stocks of pepper (or future contracts) at low prices and holds them in order to reduce supply and thereby increase prices.[14] A historic market crisis took place in 1935, when Mincing Lane Brokers, a large UK spice trader in London, acquired a substantive holding of pepper that they withheld artificially increasing prices to the detriment of buyers.[15] More recently, some Chinese companies have been suspected of such activity.

Producing nations have attempted to stabilize prices at a sustainable (higher) level. The International Pepper Community (IPC) includes all major producing nations, and has attempted (but never succeeded) in managing the price or production of pepper. This is hardly unique. Other cartels, including vanilla bean, nutmeg, and cardamom producers, and notably

OPEC, have tried but inevitably failed to control price and production. Interventions such as cartels, price manipulation, and market cornering have never succeeded for long, and normal market forces resume quickly.

Clearly, when the amount of pepper produced exceeds demand, the surplus must go somewhere. Farmers, traders, brokers and spice companies, individual consumers, and countries all hold stocks of pepper. Normally, pepper stocks are a buffer between timing variations in seasonal production (harvests) and continuous, year-round demand. In an ideal world, commodity stocks would be used up just in time for new production to become available, plus some "safety stock" in reserve to cover unforeseen demand spikes or poor harvests. If overproduction continues for a long time (as it did during the devastating Brazilian coffee crisis in the 1930s), producing countries (alone or in concert as a cartel) may stockpile the excess in a vain attempt to support prices. In the 1930 Brazilian coffee crisis, huge stocks of unsold coffee that had accumulated due to government-funded support prices were burned to reduce the supply, almost bankrupting the country. The Brazilian president, Getulio Vargas, committed suicide.

Liquidation of pepper stocks at prices below the cost of production is called dumping. In 2017, pepper-dumping allegations were made against Vietnamese interests for exporting surplus unsold pepper into the Indian market where prices were somewhat higher.[16] Eventually, excess stocks have to be sold with great care or be destroyed to support prices. The infamous EU butter mountain of the 1980s is an example of how careful supply management (including the sale of so-called Christmas butter at low prices to encourage holiday baking demand) over a period of twenty years was needed to reduce the surplus stock.

Commodity analysts monitor stock ratios, defined as the amount held in unsold stock divided by demand. A ratio of 60 percent means that 60 percent of world demand is being held in stock. When stock ratios are low, prices tend to go up due to fears that there is risk of a shortage, or interruptions in delivery. For example, in 2015, the stock ratio was 40 percent, and prices were at near all-time highs of more than $10,000 per ton. High stock ratios have the opposite effect. In 1991, the stock ratio was 160 percent, and prices were near an all-time low of $1,200 per ton. A stock ratio of greater than 100 percent means that more than a full year's worth of demand is available for sale, and prices tend to fall when that occurs. In 2017, the stock ratio was a comfortable 60 percent. If the rate of surplus production (seventy-seven tons per year) continues, it will bring the stock ratio to 100 percent by 2020. Further reduction in the price of pepper is not unthinkable.

Pepper Price Cycles

Consistent demand growth tempered by variable levels of supply has resulted in a price cycle. There were three time periods (1986–1991; 2000–2005, and 2015–present) when prices peaked and then declined, suggesting that there is a ten-year price cycle with price peaks going higher than the previous cycle. Other spices (ginger, nutmeg, turmeric, and garlic) as well as coffee, rubber, cocoa, and even crude oil exhibited similar price declines, followed by rebounds.

Supply Chain Effects

When faced with a fragmented supply industry (many small producers), companies may adopt a backward integration strategy. Backward integration occurs when a large buyer purchases or acquires control of its suppliers. Large spice companies like McCormick, after struggling to secure supplies from a myriad of small traders, have set up joint ventures and wholly owned trading companies in many of the spice-producing countries. Originally, the goal was price management, but now it is much more about quality.

Future contracts of pepper purchased from commodity exchanges are delivered many months later and may not meet the standard specified at the time of purchase. Nedspice, possibly the largest spice trader in the world, has opened processing plants in India and Vietnam to ensure product safety and quality. However, they have gone much further than processing. Nedspice has procurement teams in India and Vietnam that maintain close contacts with pepper farmers to ensure production and supply. The Nedspice Farmer Partnership Program organizes area farmers into groups, instructs them on how to make more money by growing better pepper, and provides them with a better price than local traders. Instead of relying on purchasing future contracts from the commodity exchanges, they offer good prices to local farmers directly, ensuring that they will continue to grow pepper in the future. The program fosters sustainable farming methods and traceability of pepper, increasingly important features of most food supply chains. Nedspice also engages in community support activities, such as rebuilding a local school and paving the playground area.[17]

Pepper for the Senses 5

PEOPLE CAN BE OBSESSED WITH the aroma, taste, and appearance of the food they eat. Many food items are insipid, meaning mild or neutral tasting, in their natural form. A great proportion of the food we eat is prepared, combined with other food items, and processed because we prefer it this way compared to its raw, natural state. People have added ingredients with little nutritional importance to make food more enjoyable and interesting. Herbs, spices, sugar, salt, lemon juice, and vinegar are only a few of the ingredients added to enhance the taste and aroma of food. Sometimes food is fermented or processed in a way that enhances taste, for example, cheeses, anchovies, olives, sauerkraut, kimchee, and smoked meats. Processes by which food is prepared affect the nutrient value of the food or play a role in its preservation. Smoking, drying, fermentation, leavening, pickling, salting, curing, and ageing are processing methods used not only to preserve food but also to affect its taste, aroma, and texture. The process of heat-treating food by cooking, frying, broiling, roasting, and so on also affects the taste, aroma, and texture of the food we eat.

In any discussion about food, it is useful to understand the rudiments of the human sensory mechanisms by which we perceive the world. Humans have five senses: sight, touch, smell, taste, and hearing. All of these play a role in how we perceive food, and there are differences in how the same food item looks, tastes, and smells between individuals. The French expression *à chacun son goût* (to each his own taste) reflects the diversity among different individuals with regard to food preferences. Some of the differences are hedonic, based on an individual's likes and dislikes. We all know of someone that hates some kind of food or other. Sometimes they don't like the taste; other times they have an association with a food item that is unpleasant.

Sometimes it is just the thought of the food that people find revolting: the Inuit enjoy *maktaaq*, raw frozen seal blubber; the Maasai take blood from their cows and mix it with milk (a kind of bloody milkshake). Blood puddings revolt many Canadians and Americans, and yet these are popular throughout most European countries. Large insect larvae eaten alive are a common food item among natives in the Amazonian basin. Differences in preferences can be cultural as well. For some groups, certain foods can be taboo. For example, Jews, Muslims, and a few Christian groups (including Seventh Day Adventists and the members of the Ethiopian Orthodox Church) are admonished not to eat pork. Observant Hindus and vegetarians who believe in the sanctity of sentient life do not eat meat.

Variations in the Senses

Aside from hedonic and cultural differences in food preferences, people are vastly different in their ability to sense the attributes of foods. As humans approach old age, their ability to hear, see, smell, and taste declines, explaining why many seniors do not enjoy food as much as they did in their prime or complain that food is bland tasting when it is not. Injury or illness can temporarily or permanently diminish or eliminate our senses. This can be due to common viral infections (such as a cold or flu), brain injuries (particularly orbital-frontal concussion), and exposure to chemicals. You need to be careful about what you put up your nose! It is common knowledge that cocaine damages the sense of smell. Did you know that three versions of a nasally administered homeopathic cold remedy containing zinc were found to permanently damage the sense of smell?[1]

There are substantive genetic variations in the human population with respect to the physical ability to see colors, feel, smell, hear, and taste. This means that regardless of whether or not you like a food item, what you taste or smell can be different from what someone else tastes or smells. By some estimates, up to a third of the population are unable to detect one or more sensory attributes.[2] For example, 8 percent of men and 0.5 percent of women with Northern European ancestry are red-green color blind. It has been estimated that there are approximately five million Americans affected by the loss of taste and smell. Congenital differences in sensory ability cannot be remedied and are permanent. Flavor, the combination of taste and smell, is the most important component of the enjoyment of food.

Ageusia, the complete inability to taste is rare, but *hypogeusia*, the partial loss of taste is common. As many as 30 percent of all humans do not have the full set of approximately thirty genes responsible for bitterness detection. This means that even for the same person, the perception of bitterness is likely to vary from one kind of food to another, depending on the particular compound that triggers the bitterness perception. Of course, differences in bitterness perception will also vary greatly from one individual to another. This can easily be demonstrated by giving PTC test papers (a small slip of paper impregnated with phenylthiocarbamide (PTC), a bitter-tasting compound) to a group of people. Several (two or three in a group of ten tasters) will not taste anything at all.[3] Hypogeusia can affect any number of the five tastes (sweet, salty, sour, bitter, and umami) humans can detect. In some cases, individuals may suffer from *dysgeusia*, a condition where taste is distorted or altered. Drugs used in the treatment of cancer and asthma, as well as a dietary zinc deficiency, can cause dysgeusia. There is evidence that a significant proportion of multiple sclerosis sufferers experience partial (hypogeusia) or complete (ageusia) loss of taste.

While this discussion of sensory ability sounds like a lot of bad news, about 25 percent of people (mostly women) are "supertasters" with an enhanced ability to taste food items. Researchers have been unable to determine all the reasons for the enhanced ability to taste; many supertasters appear to have more taste buds than the general population. Diagnostic tests to see if someone is a supertaster or not are based on bitterness detection. Test kits containing PTC, thiourea, and sodium benzoate test papers with testing instructions are readily available from online suppliers. Taste is a relatively simple sense, limited to five taste categories. The sense of smell is vastly more complex.

You may have noticed that different people will smell the same things quite differently or not smell anything at all. The inability to smell anything at all is called *anosmia*. A person with *hyposmia* has a reduced ability to smell, and those with *hyperosmia* have an enhanced ability to smell. To make things even more interesting, some people have a condition called *phantosmia*, a kind of sensory hallucination that causes them to smell aromas that are not actually present.[4] UPSIT (University of Pennsylvania Smell Identification Test) commercially available from Sensonics International can be self-administered. The UPSIT test consists of forty "scratch-and-sniff" encapsulated odors in different intensities that together with a scoring and interpretation manual enable users to evaluate the degree of anosmia they may suffer from.

The brain–smell relationship is so strong that smell tests have been used since the 1980s as a preliminary diagnosis of the existence of brain injuries and personality disorders. Smell tests can also be useful in the diagnosis of Huntington's disease, Korsacoff's syndrome, schizophrenia, brain tumors, AIDS, and multiple sclerosis. Phantosmia is often associated with depression, bipolar disorder, psychotic disorders, brain tumors, and Parkinson's disease.

Beyond the physical reasons for differences in flavor perception, individuals have varying abilities to recall, describe, and communicate what they experience through their sensory organs. Human beings find it particularly difficult to recall or identify odors accurately. Training of the palate using reference aromas can help, and aroma kits are available to support the training process. Ann Noble, a sensory chemist at the University of California at Davis, developed the wine aroma wheel, a graphic chart that helps wine tasters identify the aromas found in wine with greater precision. Aroma wheels are diagrams. A wheel typically consists of a group of three concentric circles. Aroma wheels work by categorizing aromas broadly in the center of the wheel, becoming more specific as you progress outward toward the edge. For example in Dr. Noble's wine aroma wheel, the center of the wheel has eleven broad categories of aromas, including herbs and leaves, vegetative, sweet, nutty, woody, earthy, oxidized, microbiological, spicy, floral, and fruity. Let's say a taster believes an odor is best identified as fruity. Then the taster proceeds outward from fruity to the middle circle of the wheel. In the middle of the wheel under the category of fruity, there are six subcategories (citrus, berry, tree fruit, tropical fruit, melon, and preserved fruit). If the berry fruit is the best description, the taster goes to the names of specific berry fruits on the outermost edge of the aroma wheel. All of the aromas presented in the wheel are found among different wines. Aroma wheels enable the evaluator to "zero in" and find the description that best fits the aroma of the product in a step-wise manner. Aroma wheels for many items have been developed[5]; however, as yet there is no aroma wheel for pepper or, more broadly, spices.

Laboratories that specialize in sensory evaluation of foods screen their tasters for sensory acuity, repeatability, and precise descriptions of their observations. Modern technology has provided researchers with instruments that exceed the ability of humans to perform sensory evaluations of food. Scientists use gas chromatography (GC) and mass spectroscopy (MS) to identify volatile and semi-volatile compounds responsible for the aromas found in foods. While GC is very good at identifying the chemicals that humans sense as odors, a hybrid technology called GC-olfactometry combines the chemical information gained from gas chromatography with the sensory information provided by the human sensory system. Touted as the most powerful odor assessment tool, GC sniffing machines are used to identify and put names to odorant components found in a variety of consumer products, environments, and residues (such as explosives, drugs, or toxins). Computer algorithms have been developed that are particularly good at mapping chemical odors onto words (for example, green banana or strawberry odors).

The Senses Work Together

Even knowing that there are differences in the human ability to sense the attributes of foods, most people appreciate and enjoy the foods they eat despite these differences. All of the senses play a role in the enjoyment of food, individually and in combination with each other. It is wonderful that all of the organs associated with our senses are present in close proximity to the mouth. The senses deliver a wide spectrum of sensations before, during, and after food is consumed. Some senses are interconnected with each other physically. The nose is internally connected with the throat, esophagus, and windpipe, which provide sensations of touch as well as smell. Other senses are neurologically connected in the brain, particularly the sense of smell and taste. Flavor is defined as the combination of aroma and taste. In almost every situation, we experience input from all the senses at the same time. Why "almost" and not in every situation? Because we can manipulate our sensory inputs. For example, you can dip the tip of your tongue into wine to assess sweetness,[6] taste wine blindfolded so you can't see if it is red or white, or plug your nose to taste something without smelling it. The senses of smell and taste are neurologically linked in the brain, and thus the perceptions of taste and smell are often confounded.[7] Surprisingly, some things we sense as tastes are actually smells. If you plug your nose and taste some pure cinnamon powder, it has almost no taste at all. If you release your nose, the cinnamon aroma presents as a taste.

Some of our sensory organs are multifunctional. A simple experiment demonstrates how the eyes contribute to the sensation of touch. If you peel a small fresh onion, eyes become irritated and tears flow to help eliminate the unpleasant, burning sensation. If you wear some kitchen goggles (that do not cover the nose), the smell of the onion does not trigger the eye irritation, proof that the eyes are instruments of touch as well as sight.

The old adage that "people eat with their eyes" is widely acknowledged by chefs, food stylists, and food photographers, who go to great lengths to make food as visually attractive as possible. Not only the food but also the presentation, which includes tabletop architecture (plates, cutlery, linens, decorative items) and composition (variation in color, shape, and height) stimulate interest, appetite, and anticipation of food quality. The term "food porn," coined in 1978, recognizes the pleasure individuals take in just looking at pictures of food.

Sounds contribute to our enjoyment of food, for example, the sound of crunchy potato chips, biting into a crisp apple, fajitas sizzling in the pan, the effervescent sound of soft drinks, or soup boiling in a hotpot all contribute to the enjoyment of our food. In Western culture, eating noises are carefully suppressed because they are considered ill mannered and gauche. However, in some Asian cultures, slurping, lip smacking, belching, and other eating sounds are indications of appreciation that the food is good and is being eaten enthusiastically with great enjoyment. Suppression of eating noises in these situations is insulting to the hosts, who derive pride and pleasure from offering the best available food to their guests.

Having noted the contribution of sight and sound in the enjoyment of food, the sensory evaluation of food is dominated by the gustatory senses of smell, taste, and touch. On the molecular level, the mechanism that allows us to taste and smell are like keys and locks. The lock is the sensory detector; the key is the molecule that fits the lock. It is the shape of the molecule that unlocks the taste sensation. That is why certain molecules will trigger some sensory responses and not others. If the molecule doesn't fit the detector, no sensation is experienced. Odorant molecules are conveyed by airflows to the olfactory epithelium located about seven centimeters above each nostril. Called the olfactory patch, the olfactory epithelium is an area about the size of a dime where odorant molecules are detected. Researchers have determined that the olfactory patch is actually an extension of the brain that protrudes into the nasal cavity, providing a very direct route between the sensory neurons and our perception of the aroma. This is quite different from sight, sound, taste, and touch, where sensory organs transmit detections via nerves to the brain where the perception takes place. The olfactory patch is truly amazing. The human olfactory patch has over one thousand different neurons, each capable of detecting a different smell.

Air conveys aromatic molecules to the olfactory patch in two different ways, both of which play an important role when we eat food. Taking in air through the nose by inhaling or sniffing draws odorant molecules directly past the olfactory patch. Smells outside the body (such as smoke, flowers in bloom, perfume, food being prepared, or aromas in the proximity of the head) are detected this way. Humans and other animals have learned to survey smells in the environment by sniffing. A secondary pathway between the throat, mouth, and nose (called retro-nasal) conveys odorant molecules released after food is ingested by means of the air being exhaled. The warm, moist, aroma-laden air moves in the reverse direction, past the olfactory patch and out through the nose. Unless the nose is plugged, even small amounts of air convey plenty of aromatic molecules past the olfactory patch. Retro-nasal aromas are often different and sometimes stronger than those obtained by breathing in through the nose. The warmth of the mouth and chewing releases more of the aromatic molecules present in the food. The olfactory patch neurons fatigue easily and the intensity of the aromas decrease rapidly after the first sniff. Anyone who has cleaned animal stables (or the cat box) knows that after the first few unpleasant minutes, the aroma of the manure decreases (thankfully) to a level where it is no longer noticeable. The sense of smell returns to normal sensitivity levels after a few minutes of breathing clear air.

Taste is a gustatory sensation that is detected by taste buds found primarily in the mouth and, to a lesser extent, in the throat and epiglottal area. In the earlier part of the twentieth century, humans were thought to be limited to only four tastes (sour, salty, sweet, and bitter); however more recently, researchers have largely agreed that there is a fifth taste, umami (sometimes described as savoriness or "meatiness"). Scientists consider umami to be a taste because it is sensed by means of special receptor cells that are different from those that detect sour, salty, sweet, and bitter components in food.

Thousands of small bumps called papillae are visible on the front, back, and sides of the tongue. Two-thirds of these are filiform papillae that have no function in the sensing of tastes. Filiform papillae provide a rough surface on the tongue that is instrumental in rasping away and retaining small amounts of foods that are licked, for example, ice cream cones or candies. A white coating on the tongue (which can turn black over time if not removed) is material that the tongue has accumulated from the inside the mouth and not been rinsed, brushed, or scraped away. Dentists say that halitosis (bad breath) is often due to bacteria growing among the food particles trapped by filiform papillae and recommend the use of tongue scrapers to dislodge and remove them.

The other papillae (fungiform, foliate, and circumvallate) are the gustatory papillae, and as a group are credited with the detection of taste in food. Each of the gustatory papillae contains several hundred taste buds, composed of fifty to one hundred taste receptor cells. Each of the five tastes has a particular type of receptor cell. In addition to the large number of taste buds found on the top, sides, and back of the tongue, a few taste buds are found in the throat and the sides and roof of the mouth. Saliva conveys molecules in the food that trigger various taste receptor cells. The brain interprets and presents these stimuli as tastes. Saliva washes away the molecules and refreshes the mouth for the next morsel of food. Some molecules that are captured by filiform papillae on the tongue or lingering in tooth crevices result in the phenomenon known as aftertaste. Aftertaste evolves in the mouth for a period of time that varies from a few seconds to several minutes in duration. Some molecules are swept away by saliva or drinks (such as dry white wine) faster than others, and thus aftertaste sensations evolve and fade over time. Aftertaste varies by quality, length of time, and intensity. Sour liquids cause an increase in salivation that improves the efficiency with which taste molecules are cleansed from the tongue and eliminated from the receptor cells. Foods such as bread can be used to absorb or mop-up molecules that are not soluble in saliva. Bread is very effective in alleviating the fiery hotness due to capsaicin, the oil present in chili peppers. Tuscan bread, traditionally made without salt, is particularly useful for this task due to its neutral flavor.

"Mouthfeel" is the term applied to the sense of touch as found in the mouth. The buccal cavity (mouth) has number of free nerve endings that sense physical and chemical properties and transmit these to the brain through the trigeminal nerves. Mouthfeel encompasses a wealth of different sensations that take place during ingestion, mastication, and swallowing. We are able to sense the texture of food, such as gritty, granular, liquid, viscous (thin or thick), soft or hard, and slippery or greasy. The mouth also has the ability to sense temperature, pain, burning, numbness, astringency, and metallicness. Astringency is often associated with the taste of bitterness but is also described as puckering sensation felt in the mucous membranes. Metallicness is an oral sensation that often occurs when a metal implement such as a stainless-steel fork comes into contact with silver fillings and produces a galvanic electrical current.

In some cases, mint or basil can induce sensations of coolness, even though the food is not cool.[8] Cloves and Sichuan pepper (recall the toothache tree) present as tingling numbness.

The Chemistry of Taste

The root of the word *pungent* is the Latin verb *pungere*, which means to pierce, prick, or sting. Pungent ingredients in food provide an unmistakable sensation when ingested by mouth. Even though pungency presents as a taste, it does not qualify as a taste because it is not sensed by the taste buds. Pungency is sensed by TRPV1 (transient receptor potential vanilloid type 1) receptors responsible for pain and burning sensations. The TRPV1 receptor is an important component of the body's heat and pain regulation system. TRPV1 receptors are located in the mucous membranes throughout the body, including eyes, nail beds, and breaks in the skin. Triggering TRPV1 receptors causes the release of endorphins, the so-called pleasure molecule: perhaps a partial explanation of the popularity of "hot" foods seasoned with chilies.

There are hundreds if not thousands of chemical compounds that are able to produce pungent sensations in humans. Among the pungent compounds found in food ingredients are capsaicin (chili peppers), piperine (black, white, red, and green pepper corns), alicine (garlic), eugenol (cloves), gingerol (ginger), cinnamaldehyde (cinnamon), allyl isothiocyanate (mustard, wasabi, horseradish), and polygodial (Mountain pepper). It is interesting to note that the compound *hydroxy alpha sanshool* contained in Sichuan pepper has a numbing/tingling effect in the mouth and is not considered to be pungent by some researchers. Sichuan pepper is called the "toothache tree" in China for its ability to numb pain. While Europe was not devoid of seasonings that provided pungency (for example, garlic), pungency occurs with far greater diversity among the spices of Southeast Asia.

The source of the pungency in capsicum (chili peppers) is capsaicinoids, a group of five vanilloid compounds produced by glands on the placenta (flesh) of the pods. Capsaicin is the most abundant and powerful of the five vanilloids. The area of highest concentration of capsaicinoids is the white pith of the inner wall, where the seeds are attached. Other parts of the plant produce these compounds to a much lesser degree; however, capsaicinoids are absorbed into the seeds due to their proximity to the flesh of the plant. Humans can detect levels of capsaicin as low as ten parts per million. Despite the strong neural sensation, chili peppers do not cause any physical or tissue damage.[9] Many regular users develop a tolerance because the TRPV1 receptors become depleted over time. It has also been found that stimulation of these receptors causes the brain to produce endorphins, the body's natural painkillers, which also induce a sense of well-being and pleasure.

Scoville Heat Units (SHU), named after its creator, pharmacist Wilbur Scoville in 1912, measures the perception of hotness. An exact weight of dried chili pepper is dissolved in alcohol to extract the capsaicinoids and then diluted in a solution of sugar water. Decreasing concentrations of the extracted capsaicinoids are given to a panel of five trained tasters, until at least three of them can no longer detect the heat. The heat level is based on this dilution, rated in multiples of 100 SHU. The procedure to determine the number of Scoville Heat Units is affected by many factors, including the capsaicin sensitivity of the taster and sensory fatigue. Measurements done by independent laboratories can vary by as much as 50 percent.

The source of pungency in peppercorns is piperine. Piperine occurs in two forms, called stereoisomers, that are chemically identical but different in shape. Chavicine is the stereoisomer of piperine that stimulates the TRPV1 receptors enabling us to sense pungency. In its other form, piperine is undetected and nearly "tasteless." On average, whole black peppercorns contain about 10 percent piperine by weight. When pepper is fresh, most of the piperine is in the form of chavicine. The loss of pungency of pepper (particularly ground pepper) is attributed to the slow transformation of chavicine into piperine, hence the importance of freshness when buying pepper. Storage and processing play a role. The isomeric transformation takes places more slowly at cool temperatures and in the absence of light. Grinding peppercorns (or anything else for that matter) generates heat. High-quality ground pepper can be produced only by a cryo-grinding process, which takes place at cold temperatures, minimizing the loss of chavicine. In the rest of this book (and in most of the literature about pepper), piperine refers to the stereoisomer chavicine.

Capsaicin does not have a naturally occurring isomer and thus does not lose its pungency over time. Piperine is not nearly as hot as capsaicin. Pure piperine is approximately 100,000 SHU, whereas pure capsaicin is 16,000,0000 SHU. Aside from pure potency, the organoleptic difference between capsaicin and piperine is the onset and duration of the heat sensation. The onset of pungency from piperine peaks quickly and fades quickly. The capsaicin burn takes longer to get started and fades very slowly. As you ingest capsaicin-bearing foods, the pungent sensation is incremental (gets hotter as you eat more), becomes invasive, and lingers in the mouth for a long time after consumption ceases. Foods seasoned with pepper are pungent at the moment they are being consumed, then the pungency diminishes quickly thereafter.

The chemical composition of piperine is similar to capsaicin.[10] Both have very low volatility and thus are odorless. Chili peppers typically do not have an aroma. However, peppercorns have both a pungent taste and a noticeable, pleasant aroma described as fresh, sharp-woody, spicy, warm, and piquant. The aroma is due to the volatility of its essential oil, which consists of a complex combination of molecules, including piperine, that can be extracted from the peppercorns by a steam distillation process. In the first stage of this process, ground black pepper is infused into a solvent such as acetone, ethanol, ethyl acetate, or ethylene dichloride. In the second stage, the essential oil is recovered by steam distillation and the subsequent solvent extraction. The amount of residual solvent is strictly limited by laws in the jurisdiction where the essential oil will be sold. A less toxic method of obtaining the essential oil is by supercritical fluid extraction (SFE). This process uses carbon dioxide gas in a high-pressure environment. Although considerably more complicated, SFE is inert, nontoxic, non-corrosive, and nonflammable and does not pollute the environment. It is the same process used to make high-quality caffeine-free coffee beans.

Sensory appreciation of pepper is complex. The heat felt by TRPV1 receptors, the aroma sensed by the olfactory patch, and flavors revealed by taste buds all play a role in how we perceive the taste of pepper. However, pepper is not eaten by itself. It is consumed in concert with the tastes and smells of food items in a wonderful symphony of sensations.

Growing Pepper

6

AFTER READING THIS CHAPTER, you will appreciate how difficult it is to be a pepper farmer. Previously, you learned how prices can fall dramatically in just a few harvests and that landowners, traders, and bankers take their share, leaving the growers with barely enough to feed their families. It is true that things will turn around; prices will go up and relative prosperity returns. But that won't help if a few bad years wipe you out. The difficulties don't end there. The grower's plants are under attack by molds, insects, and nematodes that can reduce yields by half or kill off the vines. Fertilizers and chemical and biological defenses are expensive, even when prices are low. Growing pepper is a year-round, labor-intensive endeavor. Planting, pruning, fertilizing, weeding, harvesting, processing: there isn't a day when there's nothing to do. Why anyone would want to grow pepper is not a mystery because it remains the best crop alternative among a pitiful selection of alternatives.

The *Piper nigrum* vine can be found growing almost everywhere in the southern part of India. Vines are seen growing along streets, in parks, in peoples' yards, gardens—virtually anywhere there is some kind of support for it to cling to. It still grows wild in the virgin forests of the Western Ghats mountain range in significant quantities. Long ago, pepper was gathered from vines that simply grew wild in pepper forests called *menasukans*. In areas where the conditions were particularly good (such as the Western Ghats), wild pepper grew in profusion, and supplies could be easily obtained in substantial quantities by foraging. In other areas where conditions were less favorable, the vines were fewer and produced small crops of peppercorns, often of poor quality. Even here, local inhabitants are able to able to obtain enough pepper to meet their own needs and some extra for trading. Foraging for pepper in the menasukans began to take place on a commercial scale when international trade in pepper began four thousand years ago. Local people in the Uttara Kannada district near Goa collected wild pepper for commercial purposes as late as 1801. In spite of the prodigious demand for pepper, its cultivation was mostly confined to the accessible lowland and midland regions of Kerala. The hills of the Western Ghats were left largely unmolested until about half a century ago. By the late 1960s, the present-day pepper boomtowns in Idukki district, from Kumily to Thodupuzha on either side of the Idukki reservoir,[1] were full of pepper enclaves where ambitious settlers began their hard struggle with nature and the stubbornly difficult *Piper nigrum* vine.

In the early times, the wild vine existed in balance with the other plants, animals, and insects in its immediate environment. Outbreaks of molds, diseases, and pests that lived off the vines tended to be patchy rather than pandemic. Diseases and pests would die out along with the more susceptible vines, and a few years later the vine grew back. The detritus of the varied jungle biomass fell to the ground constantly, replenishing and building up the rainforest soil. However as more and more of the virgin rain forests were cut down for wood and farmland, wild pepper was harder to find and took longer to collect. People started cultivating the *Piper nigrum* vine to obtain large amounts of pepper more conveniently without having to gather it in the jungle. Over time, when farming took the place of foraging, concentrated vine plantings fostered the rapid spread of pests and disease and depleted nutrients in delicate rainforest soils. The expedient solution was to plant the vine on fresh, new land. People emigrating from India to Indonesia and other parts of Southwest Asia were knowledgeable about how and where to plant the vine, and took cuttings with them. Before long, *Piper nigrum* was introduced to many areas with a tropical monsoon climate.

The first scientific record of *Piper nigrum* was in 1678 by a botanist named Hendrik Adriaan van Rheede in *Hortus Indicus Malabaricus*. Rheede was a Dutch administrator with the VOC in Malabar. Unlike many other Dutch commanders, who were partial to the use of military force, Rheede favored negotiation and was well liked by the local rulers. An avid naturalist, he employed twenty-five people at various times to scientifically document important plants native to the Malabar region, including five plants in the Piperaceae family (*Piper nigrum* and *Piper longam* among them). Linnaeus (1753) identified seventeen related plants forming the piper family. Also known as the founder of modern taxonomy, Linnaeus paid a great compliment to Rheede, indicating his work was one of only three naturalists that he trusted to be accurate. Subsequent taxonomists continued to map out the piper family of plants. The first major study on Piperaceae in the Indian subcontinent, *Flora of British India* (1886), divided the piper genus into six subgroups, some of which continue to be used in more recent plant classification systems. James Sykes Gamble joined the Imperial Forest Department in the latter part of the nineteenth century. The Imperial Forest Department had been established by the British to take control of the exploitation of the forest resources of India. Eventually, Gamble became the director of the Imperial British Forestry School. Over his thirty-year career, he became expert in the plants of southern India. Until his death in 1925, he spent his last years writing and rewriting *Flora of the Presidency of Madras*, a catalog of every known plant species including *Piper nigrum* in its various forms. Since that time, Indian botanists have led the way for the definition and organization of the piper family of plants beginning with Rama Rao, in his (1914) work on the "Flowering Plants of Travancore." At one time, Travancore had been a kingdom comprising the pepper-producing southern districts of Kerala and neighboring Tamil Nadu to the east. The language of Travancore, Malayalam, is still widely spoken in the region.

Piper nigrum belongs to the class of plants called angiosperms. Angiosperms are flowering plants that produce seeds within some kind of enclosure commonly called a fruit. The fruit of the *Piper nigrum* plant is a drupe: a single seed inside a fruit, not unlike a cherry or plum except much smaller. *Piper nigrum* is a perennial climbing, branching vine with a smooth, woody, articulate stem and broad, shiny green, pointed leaves. The vine grows about ten meters long and climbs upward on a host plant (or armature) using adventitious aerial roots to attach and surround the supports. *Piper nigrum* is an understory plant that requires some shade.

The main stem of the vine has nodes about ten centimeters apart. Each node produces a leaf and a flower spike: a solitary, downward-hanging, unbranched stalk twelve to fifteen centimeters long. About fifty to sixty flowers form on each spike. Each flower produces a single, spherical fruit up to six millimeters in diameter. Lateral stems (called shoots) emanate from a node on the previous year's growth. This year's shoots become next year's stems. The shoots have immature nodes that will produce leaves only, followed by leaves and flowers (which become fruits) in the following year. Stems growing away from the main trunk are called laterals. Some nodes on last year's growth produce adventitious roots that attach the plant to its support. Adventitious roots placed in contact with soil auto-convert to nutrient-absorbing roots. Pruning the tips of the vine encourages the formation of shoots and laterals. After three years of pruning and branching out, the plant has developed enough stems with leaf and flower spikes to yield a harvest.

Most of the South Indian pepper plants found in the wild are dioecious, meaning that male and female reproductive structures are located on different plants and pollinators are necessary to produce fruits. Cultivated forms of the *Piper nigrum* plant are bisexual and capable of self-fertilization. The wild dioecious plants have a greater potential for allogamy (auto crossing). Allogamy leads to the generation of variations among the *Piper nigrum* plants produced. By the process of natural selection, plants that are more disease and drought resistant have a greater chance to survive. Over a long period of time, wild pepper evolved to become largely disease free.

The history of plant breeding goes back several thousands of years. Babylonians and Assyrians pollinated the date palm artificially as early as 700 BCE. Early plant breeders interfered with the process of evolution by choosing plants that exhibited desirable characteristics and breeding them with each other. The process of vegetative propagation using cuttings or grafting enabled plants with desirable characteristics to be duplicated (cloned) without further genetic changes that occur from sexual reproduction (by seeds). Greek and Roman writings indicate that grafting was widely practiced the Mediterranean region by the fifth century BCE.[2]

Gregor Mendel's pea plant experiments from 1856 to 1863 formed the basis of modern genetics, even though it took thirty years for his work to be rediscovered. Thereafter, plant breeding became more scientific and outcome focused. Agricultural colleges were established under British rule in India at Kanpur, Pune, Sabour, Llyalpur, and Coimbatore between the years 1901 and 1905. The newly rediscovered science of Mendelian genetics was taught to young Indian plant breeders, and new hybrids slowly became available to farmers. Plant breeding and the development of modern agricultural methods had a slow start, despite the British establishment of agricultural colleges and research stations. The First and Second World Wars, followed by India's tumultuous transition to independence, delayed the improvement of agriculture. Today all that has changed. India is unquestionably the world's leader in pepper farming research and education.

The commercialized, carefully bred *Piper nigrum* strains developed to produce more and better pepper are sadly susceptible to many diseases. Modern cultivar research and development is dedicated to the development of high-yield commercial cultivars that inherit the disease resistance of their wild cousins. The major challenge facing modern pepper farmers is control of diseases, followed by optimization of profits from crop yields.

Agricultural production systems differ from natural growth in one fundamental aspect. There is a net outflow of soil nutrients by crop harvests in agricultural systems; however, there is no such thing in the natural (wild) growth of plants. Minerals lost to the physical effects of soil erosion and water leaching are continually replenished by the weathering of rocks and primary minerals in the immediate area and depositions by wind and rain of minerals originating in other regions. The crucial element of sustainability is the nutrient factor, the so-called nourishing earth, which has been shown to be the least resilient component of the soil. Plant nutrients are replenished naturally or by the addition of fertilizers. Two major approaches to agricultural production are based on the difference between natural and human soil-nutrient replenishment mechanisms.

The so-called Green Revolution is a high-input technology that uses special, high-yield cultivars supported by artificial fertilizers and agrichemicals to increase the output per hectare of land. The goal is twofold: plant efficiency and planting density. Plant efficiency is the development of plants that produce a higher proportion of crop material and less wasted biomass (leaves, stems, and roots). The second is to increase the number of these plants grown per hectare of land. Research funded by the Rockefeller Foundation and the Ford Foundation, as well as many government agencies, led to the development of new varieties of rice and other basic food crops that simultaneously maximized harvest production and minimized the growth of plant structures that were inedible. The Green Revolution, attributed to American scientist and Nobel Laureate Norman Borlaug, began in Mexico in the 1940s with a new strain of wheat. The inedible above-ground plant structures such as stems and leaves are ploughed into the soil after harvest but do not contain sufficient plant nutrients to replenish the soil. Without fertilizer, the new plant varieties exhaust the natural reservoir of soil nutrients within one or two seasons. The key requirement of the Green Revolution is fertilizer. Newly developed high-yield plants will not grow without the application of chemical fertilizers. Farmers who cannot buy fertilizers are unable to survive using the new plants.

The new plant development process has accelerated as genetic engineering has moved out of the laboratory into the field. Large biotechnology firms are continuously developing plants that are more efficient. The practice of high-density mono-crop planting has made land use and mechanical harvesting efficient. Everything ripens at the same time. New plants bred for maximum yield are not necessarily resistant to diseases and pests. Diseases and pests will run amok through large, high-density mono-crop plantings of a cultivar without natural resistance unless managed with pesticide and fungicide applications.

All plants need water to grow. Another cornerstone of the Green Revolution was irrigation. Irrigation was a way to grow high-density crop plantings in areas where water was insufficient or unfavorably distributed throughout the growing season. This opened up large dry regions that previously could not support food crops. Due to the substantial cost of the irrigation infrastructure, high-density planting makes sense.

The Green Revolution quickly spread to many countries around the world since Borlaug's groundbreaking work. It has the effect of producing many more calories per hectare of land and is credited with saving millions of people from famine. Despite the high level of food production, the Green Revolution has been criticized for supporting the overpopulation of the world. Others decry the loss of many species of plants that are no longer grown. At one time, there were over thirty thousand kinds of rice planted in India: now there are only ten kinds. The story is similar for many other food crops around the world.

The antithesis of high-input agriculture is low-input farming technology. Low-input farming is one of the cornerstones of sustainable agriculture. Like the high-input Green Revolution, sustainable agriculture also depends on the pool of nutrients in the soil. A useful analogy is that both naturally occurring and added nutrients in the soil are a capital asset. Efficient soil-nutrient management is analogous to maximizing the profit from this asset in such a way that there is no erosion of the capital. Understanding the relationship between the nutrient pool and the harvest yield must lead to meaningful practices at the farm level. For annual crops such as grains or vegetables, crop rotation plans are an important tool in sustainable farm management.

Growing the same crop year after year depletes some nutrients more than others. Eventually, yields diminish. A good crop rotation plan consists of planting a different crop in the next growing season that draws on different nutrients or replenishes nutrients used by the previous crop. For example, legumes restore nitrogen to the soil; after harvest, the remains of the plant function as a green manure. In addition, crop rotation mitigates the buildup of pathogens in the soil and pest populations. However, for perennial plants like pepper that have a life of twenty-five years or more, crop rotation is not an option. In a sustainable pepper-farming context, the best alternative to crop rotation is the simultaneous growth of multiple crops with different nutrient requirements on the same land. For example, growing ginger, turmeric, and galangal (also known as Thai ginger) side by side among *Piper nigrum* vines in pepper gardens sustains the pepper crop yield by returning necessary nutrients to the soil. In addition to improving the peppercorn yield per plant, multi-crop planting strategies provide the grower with a diversification of income and reduces the impact of commodity price variations.

The first requirement of a pepper plantation is selecting the right growth environment. *Piper nigrum* grows successfully between 20° north and 20° south latitudes. It needs a warm, humid climate with 1,250–2,800 mm of well-distributed rainfall per year. A minimum of 70 mm of rain within twenty days is needed to trigger leaf and flower spike development. Thereafter, continuous light rainfall is needed until flowering has concluded. During this crucial period, a dry spell even for a few days results in a substantial reduction in yield. A period of relatively dry conditions lasting at least a month after flowering is ideal for fruit set, although a prolonged period without any rain is unfavorable for plant growth.

Although the plant can tolerate a range of temperatures from as low as 10°C up to 40°C, it is most productive between 20°C and 30°C. It grows best at elevations below twelve hundred meters above sea level to take advantage of warm, drying breezes that limit temperature variation. The richest growth takes place on fertile, gently sloping land, rich in humus, with good drainage and light shade. Sloping land enhances drainage and helps prevent foot rot, pest infestation, and other diseases. Plants growing on south-facing slopes need extra shade to protect them from the scorching sun. Most pepper cultivars do better in partially shaded environments.

A variety of soil types are suitable for *Piper nigrum* plantings. Well-drained, virgin red or sandy forest loam soil that is rich in humus and slightly acidic (between 5.0 and 6.5 pH) is best. Water stagnation in the soil, even for a short period, is injurious for the plant. In the longer term, wet soils foster the establishment of disease-causing organisms. Choosing the right climate and growth environment reduces the need for irrigation, pesticide sprays, and soil amendments. Less-than-ideal soils can be amended before planting. A mixture of two parts soil, one part sand, and one part well-composted cattle manure is ideal. Soil often contains plant seeds, rhizomes, insects, and pathogens. To sterilize the soil, farmers use a process called solarization. Soil to be sterilized is spread out and covered with clear polyethylene plastic without air gaps between the soil and the plastic. The edges of the plastic sheet are weighted down and sealed with mud. Heat builds up in the bright sun, and after forty-five days, most unwanted pathogens are dead. After the plastic sheets are removed, soil should be treated with anti-fungal chemicals or VAM. VAM (vesicular arbuscular mycorrhizal) is a fungus inoculum that penetrates the roots of a vascular plant in order to help it capture nutrients from the soil. In addition to making fertilizers more effective, it suppresses fungal root infection.

Traditional, low-input, sustainable farming practices in India and other places use trees as support structures. Trees provide a shade canopy that can be adjusted by pruning. The leaves, prunings, and other plant detritus become humus on the forest floor. Trees host birds, insects, and small animals whose droppings help replenish soil nutrients without cost to the farmer. Most of the support trees have uses that go beyond the farming of pepper.

In lower elevations (less than seven hundred fifty meters), the spiny *Erythrina indica* tree (which also grows in Thailand) is often used because the leaves and prunings are particularly useful as a green manure, containing 4 percent nitrogen by weight. Called the coral tree, in full bloom its bright red flowers are like an aviary. Crows, mynah birds, parakeets, hummingbirds, bees, and other pollinators swarm around the tree to feast on the copious nectar. Thirty-centimeter green seedpods provide food for larger birds and are sometimes used as animal feed. Coral tree leaves are used to flavor curries, the bark makes a strong fiber, and the wood is easily carved.

The *Garuga pinnata* tree grows well in many Southeast Asian countries in elevations of four hundred to twelve hundred meters. The fruit (similar in size to a gooseberry) is edible and often pickled. The wood is used for construction, and a black dye is made from the leaves. *Grevilea robusta* (known as silver oak) is suitable for high-altitude cultivation. Its flowers attract bees (due to its very rich nectar), which produce excellent honey that is virtually free of potentially toxic honey fungus. Silver oak grows in all pepper-producing regions. Ardu (*Ailanthus sp.*) is also used as a support plant and is the food source for the silk moth *Samia cynthia*. The silk moth cocoons yield a silk fiber that is more durable and cheaper than mulberry silk.

Natural support trees provide substantial benefits for farmers who use traditional, low-input farming methods; however, they take three or more years to grow, doubling the time it takes for new pepper farm development. Artificial (dead) supports can also be used. Artificial structures are expensive in comparison to natural supports; however, they can be installed quickly. Wooden, metal, or concrete posts can serve as supports. In some areas, farmers construct pillars tier by tier using bricks cemented in a tight, alternating circular pattern with spaces in between the bricks for the adventitious roots to grab onto. The use of artificial support structures means that shade must be provided by artificial canopies and the benefits

Photo 6.1.   Traditional pepper plantation in the Western Ghats. J. Barth (Author)

of nutrient replenishment and other uses of the natural support plant are foregone. Artificial structures more than two meters tall must be strong enough to support harvesting with ladders that are leaned up against the structure. Sloping terrain prevents the use of stepladders or gantries.

Special artificial support structures have been developed for use as part of a high-input, Green Revolution farming strategy. The most effective structure for maximizing pepper yield is the column method developed in 2015 by ICAR—the Indian Institute of Spices Research in Kozhikode. The column is a vertical cylinder approximately thirty centimeters in diameter and two meters high made from plastic-coated wire mesh screen with a mesh size of approximately 1×1 cm. A steel post inside the wire mesh cylinder provides mechanical support. The cylinder is filled with non-soil growth medium consisting of two-thirds composted coir (coconut fiber), one-third composted worm castings, and some rooting hormone. Cuttings are planted at the foot of the column and shoots are trained upward, growth medium being added to the inside of the mesh cylinder as the vine climbs up the support. The nodes on the growing vine are attached to the outside of the cylinder with coconut fiber. Adventitious roots quickly convert to nourishing roots wherever they make contact with the growing medium. Pruning the tips of the vine promotes extensive branching and lateral shoot development, yielding a very dense plant structure that does not require shading. Due to multiple nourishing roots along its entire length, the vine absorbs nutrients and water from the growing medium at an amazing rate. Irrigation water containing dissolved fertilizer keeps the plant growing vigorously all year long. Good drainage by gravity prevents root rot. This method is so effective that the first crop of pepper can be harvested within eight months,[3] and year-round production may be possible.

Choosing the right *Piper nigrum* plant is important. The productive life of a vine is twenty to thirty years. Replanting old, worn-out vines with new cultivars is an opportunity to improve plantation performance over time. New *Piper nigrum* cultivars have been developed with different characteristics, and the choice of cultivar must be optimized for the particular situation in which it will be planted and the farming methods needed to sustain production. There are more than fifty commercialized cultivars, plus others that have persisted in pepper farming areas for centuries. Each has its own characteristics. A sampling of some modern hybrids provides an idea of what is available.

The Kerala Agricultural University developed a series of hybrid strains in their Panniyur Research Station. *Panniyur 1* was the first hybrid developed and is famous in most producing countries. It is high yielding compared to wild pepper and produces good-quality peppercorns with bold-tasting berries. *Panniyur 1* produces large berries (>4.25 mm) suitable for Tellicherry pepper production. It produces up to 1,242 kg per hectare in sunny areas and is resistant to most diseases and pests. An early ripening variety, it is ideal for white pepper. It has relatively high piperine (5.3 percent), oleoresin (11.8 percent), and essential oil (3.5 percent) content. It is not suitable for heavily shaded areas. By comparison, *Panniyur 2*, released in 1990, is ideal for shady areas, producing up to twice as much (2,570 kg per hectare annually) as *Panniyur 1*. It seems like a great choice, however, *Panniyur 2* is an alternate producer, meaning that the vine alternates between producing a big crop one year and a small crop the following year. Growers of *Panniyur 2* incur higher labor costs. The small crop is due to nutrient depletion in the plant stems and soil by the preceding large crop. Most fruit trees (apple, pear, plums, etc.) exhibit the same characteristic unless pruned and fertilized annually. The alternate crop cycle can be "smoothed" by a program of nutrient sprays applied at specific times (for example, immediately after flowering) and limiting new growth by pruning. *Panniyur 2* is ideal for black pepper production, with high piperine content (6.6 percent), oleoresin (10.9 percent), and essential oil (3.3 percent). It is susceptible to quick wilt, also known as Phytophthora root rot disease, that can cause the sudden death of the pepper vines.

Panniyur 4, another variety released by ICAR in 1990, is a regular (not alternate) producer and is well adapted to less-than-ideal growing situations (high altitude, shady, and dry). *Panchami* is a regular producer with very good crop yields (2,828 kg per hectare) that is disease and pest resistant. It is well adapted to shade and high-altitude cultivation; however, the peppercorns have lower piperine content (4.7 percent).

Most pepper farmers procure their own plant material for propagation. Propagation can be accomplished from seed or by rooting the cuttings obtained from the stem and runners of existing plants. Propagation from seed takes much longer and consequently is not a common practice. Stem cuttings are taken from vigorous, high-producing, disease-free donor plants. Lateral branches with short inter-nodal spacing are ideal. Untangling a lateral shoot that has been left to grow on its own can be time consuming and frustrating. Shoots intended for propagation are coiled on wooden pegs fastened to the plant support for several months in order to keep the new growth from attaching to the support plant and existing vine growths. Cuttings are about fifty centimeters in length below a node and should incorporate plenty of adventitious roots along their length. After the leaves have been removed, they are put into polyethylene bags with a mixture of soil, humus, nutrient, and rooting hormone until roots are established, then they are transplanted into nursery beds or pots.

A faster method developed in Sri Lanka involves digging a trench about thirty centimeters deep and forty-five centimeters wide to a convenient length. The trench is filled with a mixture of sand, soil, and manure. A ridgepole is mounted about thirty centimeters above the center of the trench for its entire length. Split bamboo or black water pipe ribs are placed with the concave side up along each side of the ridgepole (similar to rafters in a roof). The cuttings are rooted in the trench and then trained up the concave side of the split ribs. Soil is added to the split ribs as the cutting grows to encourage adventitious root production. When the vine has developed plenty of roots, it is transplanted into the pepper garden. ICAR has used their vertical cylindrical support system to make propagation faster and simpler. Runners (shoots) generate adventitious roots wherever they make contact with the soil and are simply removed from the outside of the cylinder and transplanted into pots or nursery beds. The pots containing the rooted cuttings are matured in a nursery prior to planting out in the pepper farm.

Young *Piper nigrum* vines are trained to grow in a variety of ways. Bush pepper (not to be confused with wild pepper) consists of multiple short vines planted in a bush-like shape in containers close to the ground or in shallow dish-like depressions. It is ideal for home gardening, or as an intercrop between plantings of low canopy plants such as rubber trees. It does not require ladders to harvest and is an attractive garden plant. Bush pepper yields per hectare of land are low, since the air space above the plant is not utilized. A well-maintained bush pepper plant can produce one kilogram of peppercorns per year, compared to as many as three kilograms for a vertically trained vine. Bush pepper plants in large pots are less likely to have soil pathogen problems than those planted in the ground.

Most commercial pepper growers use a vertical support structure where the vine climbs vertically off the forest floor. Small holes are dug about fifty centimeters away from the base of the support structure. Each hole is fifty centimeters square and about fifty centimeters deep. The cutting is placed in the hole and filled with a mixture of sand, soil, and manure. As the plant grows, it is trained up the support, fastened to the support with ties if necessary. Pruning the tip encourages branching out and reduces spike formation so that plant growth is more vigorous.

Shallow, dish-like depressions about seventy centimeters in diameter are formed in the soil around the base of the support structure. These depressions in the ground restrain water, fertilizers, and agrichemicals that will be applied to soil at the base of the plant from flowing away from the plant roots. The depressions are essential in areas with insufficient rainfall. Pepper farmers without irrigation hoses (drip lines) will water their plants using a bucket in times of drought.

Low-input pepper farming relies on composted vegetable matter and animal and human manure to fertilize the vines. In Cambodia, farmers place a mix of fresh soil (from land that has not been cultivated), manure, and compost at the base of the vine so that nutrients are watered into the soil below. The fresh soil in the mix provides natural nutrients and minerals that have been depleted from the base soil over time. Farmers who use high-input "Green Revolution" techniques will use chemical fertilizers, applied in liquid form by drip lines or by hand to supply the soil with nutrients.

Diseases and Pests

So far, it looks fairly easy to be a pepper grower. Get some good land, set up the support structures, plant the pepper vines, and in a few years, the harvest takes place. Unfortunately, the *Piper nigrum* vine is vulnerable to a number of diseases caused by fungi, bacteria, virus, insects, and microscopic worms called nematodes. The most serious constraint facing pepper production is diseases caused by molds and fungi. Growing pepper among crops such as banana, yams, ginger, turmeric, coffee, and cocoa crops play a role in the buildup of populations of certain pests and pathogens that reduce the production and productivity of pepper. Mono-crop pepper plantations have these problems, too.

Fungus Diseases

The major disease (particularly in India, Indonesia, and Malaysia) is *Phytophthora capsici*, also known as foot rot or quick death. *Phytophthora* is aptly named, from the Greek *phyto* (plant) and *phthora* (destroyer). It is a genus consisting of many hundreds of types. Foot rot causes root, leaf, and fruit disease on many species of plants and is found all over the world. Phytophthora most infamously was the cause of the Irish Potato Famine, which killed a million people and was responsible for the emigration of a million more. Foot rot has reduced pepper production dramatically. In Indonesia, it is estimated that a 5 percent reduction of national pepper production is due to the disease. In India, the story is worse, with some estimates as high as a 30 percent production loss.

Phytophthora is a fungus-like organism that is spread by water, wind, and rain. Infection can be aerial or through water in the soil. In the ground, *Phytophthora* attacks the roots and spreads upward to the stem, where it forms an infected collar around the base of the plant. The infected collar chokes off the flow of nutrients to the vine. Leaf yellowing, wilting, and dropping are the terminal stages of the disease. Early detection is difficult, and yellowing of the leaves usually indicates that the roots are already dead. Plants infected by soil transmission die within a few days. Aerial transmission occurs in hot, humid conditions when wind and rain transport spores found on the soil surface or the leaves of infected plants to the leaves and stems of plants nearby. Leaf and stem infection spreads from the leaves downward to the roots. Plants infected by the aerial vector can survive for several weeks, providing a rich source of spores for further aerial transmission.

The temperature and water requirements for *Piper nigrum* and *Phytophthora capsici* are the same. Both need warm temperatures and plenty of water. *Phytophthora capsici* spores can survive in warm, damp soils up to six years. In dry soils, the spores are viable for nineteen months. Infected plant material left on the plantation floor can harbor spores for two or

three rainy seasons. This makes eradication of the disease extremely difficult. If the farmer decides to plant other crops on infected soil (particularly
melons, squash, pumpkin, tomato, cucumber, macadamia nuts, vanilla, or
cocoa), they will also succumb to the disease. It is widely accepted that
Phytophthora capsici is lying dormant in many farm soils, waiting for warm,
wet conditions to activate the spores. Soil contamination with *Phytophthora
capsici* is a huge problem in Kerala. Sometimes *Phytophthora capsici* proceeds
slowly and is called slow wilt, or yellow disease (named after the yellowing
of the leaves). In this case, plants die slowly over a period of two to three
years. This disease is often seen in Malaysia.

Disease management strategies involve controlling water, pepper plantation cleanup, and soil decontamination. Traditional hillside pepper farms
on well-draining sandy loam soils are 60 percent less likely to have foot
rot infections. Adding sand to soils that retain water can help with drainage. Pepper farms on flat land need to have drainage systems in place to
avoid prolonged wet soil conditions that harbor the spores. These include
elimination of deep (more than ten centimeters) dish structures constructed
in the soil at the foot of vines to aid with irrigation. After heavy rains or
irrigation, deep dishes lead to soaked soils that support the growth and
spread of *Phytophthora capsici* spores. Watering without soaking followed
by dry periods between watering impedes the spread of the spores through
the soil. Thorough cleanup and burning of dead leaves, stems, and detritus
in areas where foot rot occurs helps confine the infection. Studies have
shown that infection spreads in a radial, centrifugal pattern away from the
infected plants.

Soils that are heavily infected with the *Phytophthora capsici* spores are
useless for growing crops. The process to eliminate *Phytophthora* from
infected soils takes a lot of hard work. Dead and dying vines must be
removed. Ploughed up soils are covered with plastic sheeting similar to
the solarization process. A minimum of 40°C for four hours a day over
twenty-eight consecutive days are required to kill the spores near the surface. Spores that are deeper can survive, so soil must be "turned" to bring
deeper spores to the top. After the soil is turned, the process is repeated
until all soil to a depth of sixty-five centimeters has been treated. After
solarization is complete, the damp sterilized soils are dried in the bright
sun. To accommodate the drying process, soils are temporarily covered
with tarps during rainy periods and turned frequently to expose deep,
damp soil to the surface sun and air. To increase sun exposure, reduction
of the shade canopy of support trees by pruning is useful. After a year of

drying, sacrificial baits (such as pepper leaf or castor seeds) are placed in the soil to test if the viable spores have been eliminated and new planting of *Piper nigrum* can take place. When replanting, farmers must ensure that the new cuttings are disease free and the use of disease-resistant cultivars is advisable. Studies have shown that pepper vines grown on natural (live) support trees have lower rates of infection than those using dead wood or concrete support systems.

There are a number of biochemical agents available to control *Phytophthora*. Two biological control agents effective in combating soil-born fungus infections are *Trichoderma* and *Pseudomonas*. *Trichoderma* is a root fungus that does no harm to the pepper vine. *Pseudomonas* is a rod-shaped bacterium. The exact process by which they work is not known; however, both have been shown to be effective against *Phytophthora* and other soil-born fungus infections. They are applied to the soil. Chemical fungicide sprays, including copper sulfate (Bordeaux mixture), can be used to inhibit infections on the aboveground plants.

Fusarium wilt (*Fusarium solani*) is another soil-born pathogen that attacks the roots. It is particularly problematic in Brazil. Fusarium infections kill the plant quickly and reduce the productive life of the plantation to six years or less after infection. As the plants die, harvests become progressively smaller until the pepper plantation is no longer economically viable. Control of Fusarium is primarily by chemical means. The symptoms of fusariosis begin at the roots and then proceed up branches, eventually resulting in falling leaves, root rot, and plant death. *Fusarium solani* can produce metabolites that are toxic to humans. Individuals who have compromised immunity are susceptible to bone (osteomyelitis) and eye (endophthalmitis) infections. During the harvest, pepper plantation workers may suffer eye irritation from dust and contact with plant material. Eye trauma allows fusarium spores in the air to enter the cornea where they grow, causing keratitis. People with HIV are particularly susceptible.

Anthracnose is a plant disease caused by *Colletotrichum necator*, often associated with greenhouse plants and grape vines in North America and Europe. Anthracnose in pepper plants, called "pollu" disease in India, must not to be confused with the pollu beetle, an insect pest that attacks pepper. Anthracnose is a fungus that affects the leaf, stems, and fruit of the pepper vine. Infected peppercorns are black or brown in color, not green. It is common in India and seems to be more common on farms that grow pepper as an intercrop with coffee. Control is by chemical sprays. No resistant cultivars have been developed.

Insect Pests

In India, researchers have identified fifty-six insect species that attack the *Piper nigrum* plant. Insects damage the plant and peppercorns by feeding. The range of insects that attack the pepper plants include shoot and leaf borers, leaf gall thrips, leaf scale, grasshoppers, leaf hoppers, white flies, aphids, mealybugs, even stink bugs. The worst losses are due to the tiny pollu beetle, *Longitarsus nigripennis*, which is indigenous to India. The incidence of pollu infestations is as high as 30 percent in Malabar. The female pollu beetle lays its eggs in small holes that it bores into the tender, unripe peppercorns and seals them in with a plug of feces. Sometimes it will lay the eggs on the bottom of a leaf or on a flower spike. The eggs hatch into creamy-white grubs that survive by eating new-growth leaves, buds, and peppercorn spikes. The hollowed-out peppercorns left behind have no value. The pollu beetle has very few natural predators. It is controlled using insecticide sprays. In recent years, many effective insecticides have been banned for use in agriculture for a variety of reasons. Pesticides are known to kill useful insect pollinators, birds, and other wildlife. Farmers who have not been well trained or equipped with personal safety equipment can inadvertently poison themselves, their families, and neighbors. Peppercorns contaminated with pesticide residues are not marketable in Western countries, where every shipment is tested. Research to find nonchemical means to fight the pollu beetle are ongoing. Wild pepper plants are remarkably resistant to pollu beetle attack. The Kerala Agricultural University at their Panniyur Research Station has developed several pollu-resistant *Piper nigrum* cultivars.

Pepper lace bug is primarily a problem in Indonesia and Malaysia; however, it is also found in the southern tip of India. Lace bug populations increase during the rainy season, although the insect can be seen throughout the year. The adult lace bugs lay eggs on the underside of leaves, and the newly hatched nymphs suck juices from the plant. Lace bug feeding is not a serious threat to plant health or survival; however, flower spike attack is the most damaging because it results in loss of fruit. The most serious consequence of pepper lace bug infestation is the spread of the PYMV virus.

Virus Infections

The most harmful virus disease is pepper yellow mottle virus (PYMV). Lace bugs, mealybugs, and infected plant material spread the virus to otherwise healthy plants. Symptoms include yellowish spots on new leaves, short spacing between nodes, and small spikes with partially hollowed berries. The vine's growth is stunted and a mosaic pattern appears on the leaves. Yield diminishes quickly, as does the quality of the crop. There is no cure; however, removal of infected plants and insect control is the best way to minimize damage.

Pepper stunt disease was discovered in Kerala in 1975. Malaysia, Indonesia, Sri Lanka, Thailand, and Brazil have also reported its presence. Stunt disease is rarely fatal for the plant; however, plant productivity is low. Ongoing research suggests that it is caused by a complex of cucumber mosaic viruses (CMV) that are spread by the transfer of sap from infected plants by knives used for grafting or taking cuttings. Even tiny amounts of sap clinging to cutting and grafting tools can spread the virus. Several countries, including Brazil, have stopped the importation of *Piper nigrum* vines in an effort to isolate the disease. Control is by sterilization of cutting tools and the eradication of infected plants and plant material.

Nematode Pests

Nematodes are parasitic roundworms found in soil that occur in many shapes and sizes. Virtually every country suffers agricultural productivity losses from nematodes. Nematodes cause damage to roots and plant tissues on their own but also in conjunction with disease-causing organisms. Damaged roots and tissues cannot absorb water and nutrients efficiently.

Root knot nematodes (*Meloidogyne spp.*) are the most destructive nematodes on the planet. They affect more than two thousand different kinds of plants and are responsible for a loss of 5 percent of the world's crops. The roots of the plant generate galls to protect itself after penetration by the nematode's larvae. The gall inhibits the absorption of water and nutrients. Young plants die, and older plants lose vigor and produce small harvests. Eventually, significant root loss kills the plant. There are a number of pesticides that can be used to defend against nematode attack; however, they are expensive and have residue and health issues for farm workers. It is impossible to eliminate all nematodes from the soil, so farmers adopt management practices to limit their damage. Neem cake, a by-product of oil extraction from neem seeds, is an organic fertilizer that also protects roots from nematodes, white ants, and soil grubs. Neem trees, related to mahogany, grow in arid tropical and subtropical zones of Asia, Africa, the Americas, Australia, and the South Pacific islands. Neem cake works best when applied consistently over time as part of a fertilizer program. Plants suffering from nematode attacks are more susceptible to fungus attacks also. It is fortunate that the same moisture-control methods used to fight fungus infections originating in the soil are also effective for nematode-infested soils.

Field Management

New plants must be shaded until root and stem systems are well established. *Piper nigrum* is a surface feeder, and roots are concentrated close to the surface. Weeds are a major problem in pepper plantations. They compete with the *Piper nigrum* vine for moisture and nutrients and are impervious to attack by most pests. Hoeing easily damages the *Piper nigrum* feeding roots, so weed control is accomplished by slashing horizontally around the base of the plant. Weeds can also be discouraged by planting cover crops or mulching. Cover crops such as *Trifolium* (a type of clover) and *Centrosema pubescens* (a legume) are an excellent alternative to mulch because in addition to discouraging weed growth, they stabilize soil moisture and contribute to the nitrogen content of the soil. Mulching with dry, pathogen-free leaves around the base of each vine helps retain moisture during dry periods. Pruning of the support trees takes place twice a year. Ideally, living supports should be pruned just before flowering in April and May to ensure the *Piper nigrum* vine receives the correct amount of sunlight for good fruit set. Pruning of the support trees is a very labor intensive task. The green matter from pruning a hectare of living support trees amounts to fifteen tons per year! Pruning from support trees such as the coral tree (*Erythrina indica*) serve a double purpose as both mulch and green manure.

Harvest

Pepper harvests take place at different times of the year. In fact pepper is being harvested somewhere in the world all the time. The crop is harvested by hand using stepladders (on flat land) or poles with alternating rungs on hillsides. The harvest time depends on the use that will be made of the crop. Green pepper that will be pickled and canned is harvested four to five months after flowering. In parts of Sri Lanka where thieves may enter a pepper plantation and steal the harvest, growers often pick their crop early. These immature berries are dried to yield an inferior quality of black pepper called "light pepper." The peppercorns are small and dark in color but light in weight. Light pepper has very high oleoresin content and is purchased by oleoresin extraction companies in India. For most uses, the harvest takes place about eight months after flowering. Pepper berries should be uniform in size, spherical, and evenly distributed on the spike. Missing berries are indicative of flowers that did not pollinate. Even on the

Table 6.1. Pepper Harvest Calendar

	Jan	Feb	Mar	Apr	May	Jun	Jul	Aug	Sep	Oct	Nov	Dec
Brazil							BW	BW	BW			
Cambodia			B	B	B	B						
Ecuador				B	B	B	B	B	B	B	B	B
India	B	B	B								B	B
Indonesia						W	BW	BW	B			
Madagascar		B	B	B	B	B	B	B	B	B		
Malaysia						B	BW	BW	BW	W		
Sri Lanka	B			B	B	B	B					B
Vietnam	BW	BW	BW	BW	BW	W	W	W	W	W	W	W

B = black pepper   W = white pepper
Source: http://www.pepperdesk.com/harvest-calendar/

same plant, not all pepper spikes ripen at the same time. Pepper must be harvested in weekly intervals over a period of one or two months, carefully selecting spikes that are at the desired point of ripeness. Immature berries shrivel up on drying and produce small peppercorns that reduce the quality of the product when sold. When the harvest is complete, any remaining spikes must be removed from the plant to encourage the next growth cycle.

When all the berries are dark green in color and easily separate from the spike by rubbing between the hands, the farmer can harvest green pepper. If one or two berries on the spike have turned orange (usually two weeks after the green stage), it is time for harvesting black pepper. After all the berries on the spike have turned red, they are harvested to make white pepper or red peppercorns.

Green peppercorns are processed in several ways. They are dried, freeze-dried, or shipped frozen to be pickled in brine and canned. Air-dried peppercorns are briefly cooked or steamed to preserve their color, then air-dried in the sun. Freeze-drying preserves the color without the hot water or steam bath. Madagascar green peppers are frozen and shipped to France, where they are pickled in salt brine and canned. Other countries also process and export pickled green pepper. Sulfur dioxide (an antioxidant) is used to preserve the green color. The use of sulfur dioxide as an antioxidant in food processing is widespread, including in beer, wine, and packed vegetable products.

The processing of black peppercorns differs from one region to another. In India, berries are removed from the spike (decorned) by trampling with bare feet or using a simple hand-operated threshing machine. The harvested spikes from pepper plantations located near busy, dusty

Photo 6.2.   Harvesting pepper in the Idduki district. J. Barth (Author)

roads must be washed in cool, clean water to get rid of dirt before decorning. The berries are plunged into boiling water for about one minute and then dried in the sun for several days. The hot water activates the phenolase enzyme that produces a rich black color and ruptures the cells in the outer skin (pericarp) accelerating the drying process. Black pepper processed this way has a slightly shiny, dark surface and commands higher prices. Other Indian producers (especially in the Wayanad district) partially dry the washed peppercorns in the sun for two days and then pack them into bags. The heat from sun warms the peppercorns, and the residual moisture retained in the bags fosters a very even fermentation. The peppercorns acquire a dark, black, slightly shiny color. The drying process is completed in the usual way.

In Indonesia, the recently harvested spikes are piled up for a few days and allowed to ferment to a brown color before decorning. The fermentation process is already complete, so no hot water blanching is performed.

Peppercorns are spread out on plastic sheets to dry in full sun for several days until the moisture content of the peppercorns is 14 percent or less by weight. The moisture content is easily measured by weighing a fixed volume of peppercorns. Lighter weights mean drier pepper.

Photo 6.3.   Drying black peppercorns on the farm. J. Barth (Author)

Photo 6.4.   Final drying to 11 percent moisture on rooftop. J. Barth (Author)

After drying, peppercorns are garbled. Garbling involves cleaning the pepper of dust and contaminants and removing stalks, pinheads (small peppercorns), white heads (black peppercorns with the pericarp detached), and broken peppercorns. This is accomplished manually by winnowing, fanning, and hand sorting. White heads are picked out by hand. Screening separates the larger (more valuable) peppercorns from ordinary sizes. Many small producers leave garbling to the village trader who buys their crop and aggregates the pepper from several growers before shipment to wholesale traders. After garbling, the density of the pepper is between five hundred and six hundred grams per liter, depending on the size of the peppercorns and moisture content.

In some areas (particularly in Indonesia, Malaysia, and Vietnam), commercial pepper processors have automated equipment to perform these tasks. Growers simply deliver the freshly harvested spikes to a processor, and the rest is done for them. In some cases, large spice trading companies who export the final product for their own needs own the processing company.

White pepper processing is more complex and labor intensive. It is also risky, because mold and hungry birds can damage or destroy the ripe crop when it is still on the vine. The fully ripe (red) peppercorns are put into mesh bags that are soaked in slow running water (usually a stream) for two weeks. The water fosters a microbial retting process (some would call it a rotting process) that separates the fruit (pericarp) from the white peppercorn seed within. The de-fruited (decorticated) berries are then put into shallow tanks and trampled with the feet to remove any remaining bits of fruit, leaving only the seeds behind. Care is taken to ensure that the seeds are not damaged. After a thorough washing, the seeds are dried until remaining water content is 14 percent (or less). Water quality plays an important role in white pepper production. Contaminated water can impart a "swampy" odor to the peppercorns. Other methods of decortication using steam or boiling water save time and are more sanitary but produce a darker-colored peppercorn with lower piperine content.

Red peppercorn processing is similar to black pepper. Fully ripe red peppercorns are sorted to ensure only perfect, undamaged fruits are used. The peppercorns are briefly immersed in boiling water, then sun-dried. Red peppercorn production is risky because any partially decayed berries will infect the crop. The fruits must dry quickly to preserve the color and prevent rot or mold from setting in. Sometimes sodium metabisulfite is added to the water bath to prevent oxidation that would diminish the bright red color.

Post-Farm Processing

After leaving the farm, dried peppercorns are sold for a variety of uses that involve further processing. The most common of these is the production of ground black pepper. Ground black pepper is convenient for domestic, foodservice, and food processor usage. The process of grinding pepper in large quantities is not as simple as it sounds. The flavor of pepper comes from its essential oils, which evaporate and oxidize when exposed to air. Oxidation of the essential oils make pepper taste and smell rancid. By reducing peppercorns into a powder, the surface area is increased, and the rates of oil oxidation and evaporation are much higher. While the aroma in a spice mill operation is wonderful, the problem is how to keep it in the pepper and not in the factory environment. To understand the complexity of the problem, it is useful to understand something about the process of turning a solid into a powder.

There are two ways to reduce large particles into small particles: crushing or grinding. Crushing works well for hard solids. Compressive force is used to fracture larger pieces into small particles. Rocks, salt, refined sugar, and wheat are reduced to a fine powder by crushing. The mechanical device used for this purpose is called a mill. Crushing on a continuous basis can be accomplished using hard rollers. Modern flourmills crush grains of wheat between a series of rollers with progressively smaller spaces until a very fine flour is obtained. Friability is the prime characteristic of the material to be crushed: the material must crack, chip, or crumble when subjected to compressive forces. The second way to reduce the size of a solid is by grinding. Grinding combines compressive, shearing forces and impact forces to break down materials into particles. In the past, wheat was made into flour by grinding it between two millstones. The sharp edges of the millstones sheared the crushed wheat kernels into powder form. This works well when the material is dry and friable. If you tried this with a potato, you would get mush. Moisture in the material to be ground cakes up and clogs the device. Both crushing and grinding create heat, although grinding creates a lot more. Large millstones were used to absorb excess heat created by grinding.

Pepper is not ground; it is crushed using a device called a hammer mill. Hammer mills (also called pulverizers) are devices that smash the solid into smaller pieces by progressively hitting it between a hammer and a platen: between a rock and a hard place, if you will. The hammer mill consists of a shaft fitted with a multi-vane rotor (the hammer) that spins inside a heavy steel cylinder with a removable cover on the front. The top half of the cylinder has grooves with sharp edges. The bottom half accepts removable steel screens of various sizes depending on desired fineness of the final product. Peppercorns are fed into the center of the mill through a chute mounted on the removable front cover. When the machine is turned on, the spinning rotor moves the peppercorns to the outside of the cylinder by centrifugal force and smashes them against the edges of the grooves. The rotor "hammers" the peppercorns onto edges of the grooves, breaking them up into pieces. Bits of smashed peppercorn small enough to pass through the screen at the bottom of the cylinder are captured in a receptacle. Larger pieces spin around repeatedly until they have been smashed to the desired size and ejected from the bottom of the mill. In general, high rotor speeds and small screen sizes produce more finely ground pepper. Slower rotor speeds and larger screen sizes produce course ground pepper. The operator's skill comes from experience and judgment with peppercorns that have natural variability in friability and moisture content. A version of the hammer mill is the pin mill (also known as a centrifugal impact mill). The pin mill reduces the size of the peppercorn by smashing it hundreds of times against stout metal pins mounted on two discs, one stationery, the other rotating at high speeds. As the disc rotates, the peppercorns are smashed repeatedly as they bounce from one pin to another. No mesh screens are needed because the size of the pepper granules is controlled by the speed of the rotating disc. Pin mills create heat to a lesser extent than hammer mills.

The pulverizing process generates heat that builds up in the mill. Studies have shown temperatures of 40°C–95°C occur, depending on the moisture and oil content of the peppercorns. This is more than enough heat to drive off the volatile oils that give pepper its wonderful aroma and taste. The problems go beyond flavor loss. Air oxidizes the heated essential oils in the ground pepper, quickly turning it rancid. The heat releases oils and moisture in the peppercorns that combine with finely powdered pepper to form a pasty solid that clogs the grooves and screens in the mill. Clogged screens cause a build-up of ground pepper in the mill, further elevating the temperature. Cooling the equipment with chilled water or cold air helps, but is insufficient for reducing the temperature of the peppercorns themselves as they are hammered to bits. In addition to cooling the mill, the peppercorns themselves must be chilled. The solution is cryogrinding. Cryogrinding uses liquid nitrogen (-195°C) to precool the peppercorns so that the heat generated can be absorbed by the time the grinding is complete. The liquid nitrogen keeps oils in a solid, crumbly (friable) state that is necessary for crushing and provides a completely dry environment that inhibits oxidation and rancidity.

Modern cryogenic grinding equipment consists of a pre-cooler and refrigerated grinding mill. The pre-cooler consists of a screw auger encased in a barrel-like tube with a hopper at one end and feeder at the other. As the auger moves peppercorns along, liquid nitrogen injected into the barrel vaporizes and lowers the temperature of the peppercorns below the brittle (friable) point of the volatile oils. To economize on the amount of liquid nitrogen used, the barrel is insulated from the environment. The mill is cooled to subzero temperatures so that pepper does not clog the machine or lose its precious volatile oils. Even the best ground pepper prepared using the latest cryogrinding technology suffers the loss of 20 percent of the essential oils found in the peppercorns. Air-tight packaging to prevent oxidization and evaporation are signs of good-quality ground pepper.

Ground pepper is sold in various grinds. A mesh screen in the bottom of the grinder controls the size of the pepper particles. Mesh size is a standard measurement system for the screens. It is based on the number of open spaces per inch on a screen. As the mesh size number increases, the particle size decreases.

Pepper Oleoresin

Unless you are involved in the commercial food processing industry, it is unlikely that you have heard of this product. Imagine that you could extract all the good taste, aroma, and color from the peppercorn and throw the remaining plant material away. That is black pepper oleoresin. It has all the flavor profiles of black pepper in a concentrated, oil-based, quick-release liquid. It is ideal for processors of foods, beverages, pharmaceuticals, and chemicals because it is so much easier to use. Pepper oleoresin is also used to make aromatic candles, soaps, and hair lotions.

Pepper oleoresin is a derivative of pepper, along with isolates like piperine and certain nutraceuticals (also called bio-active phytochemicals) used for the manufacture of medicines. Pepper oleoresin is a dark, oily liquid about the same consistency as molasses. It is sold in various quality specifications, depending on piperine (pepper essential oil) content. The higher the piperine content, the higher the price. Most of the oleoresin produced is extracted from light berry pepper that can be purchased at lower cost than black peppercorns. Light berry pepper contains about 10.5 percent oleoresin and 3.5 percent piperine. To put that into perspective, a metric ton of light berry pepper will yield 105 kg of oleoresin and a further 3.5 kg of piperine.

There are a number of different ways to extract the oleoresin and piperine from the pepper berries. Synthite, the largest producer of oleoresins in the world, uses a four-stage process. Since piperine is worth about six times as much as oleoresin, it is extracted first. The first step is to clean the peppercorns of any dirt or debris. To make extraction more efficient, the pepper is lightly crushed by passing it between steel rollers. The first stage is a process called steam distillation. Batches of about two tons of clean, rolled peppercorns are loaded into a large columnar vessel heated by injecting steam into the bottom of the column. A temperature gradient develops such that the cooler temperatures are near the top and hotter temperatures farther down the column. As steam is admitted into the column, the more volatile, aromatic components of the pepper evaporate and rise up high in the column. The less volatile components stay near the bottom of the column. Piperine, the most volatile (and most valuable) component, along with water vapor is captured and cooled in a condenser. After condensation, the water and piperine are easy to separate because the oil floats on top of the water. It takes about twelve hours for the piperine to be extracted in this way. It is not possible to extract all of the piperine: some remains in the leftover material called de-oiled pepper cake at the bottom of the apparatus. The de-oiled pepper cake is taken to the second stage of the production process, the continuous extraction plant.

The de-oiled cake is reinforced with about 25 percent additional light peppercorns to bring up the total piperine content. Oleoresin must contain some piperine. A continuous extraction plant consists of an enclosed conveyor belt with spray nozzles along its length (something like a tunnel) and a solvent recovery unit. The conveyor belt moves the reinforced de-oiled pepper cake material slowly down the length of the machine. A solvent (typically hexane, acetone, ethylene dichloride, or alcohol) is sprayed onto the pepper cake material, and it percolates through the cake and dissolves the oleoresins as it passes through the machine. After the solvents are saturated with the dissolved oleoresin and piperine, they are recovered by heating and distillation in the solvent recovery unit, leaving the crude oleoresin/piperine material behind. The solvents are reused many times. The crude oleoresins are checked for residual solvent levels by the quality control lab. At this point in the proceedings, the hot oleoresins are "gloppy," lumpy masses of hot, semi-solid oil in a liquid stew. The third stage of the process homogenizes the oleoresins into a uniformly dense, viscous liquid.

The crude oleoresins are put into a tank where they are continuously mixed by mechanical paddles as they cool to ambient temperature

(25°C–30°C). The well-mixed oleoresins are then processed in a machine called a sand mill. Sand mills use small, inert particles (such as sand) to bombard and completely separate tiny, even microscopic globs of oil into a permanently uniform liquid. When completely homogenized, the oleoresins are subjected to a battery of tests[4] and blended to the correct specification with the addition of some piperine from the first stage if necessary.

Researchers have identified non-solvent methods of oleoresin extraction. The solvents have toxic, reactive, flammable, and corrosive qualities that are dangerous to human health. Supercritical fluid (SCF) extraction using carbon dioxide gas is considerably safer, since CO_2 is harmless and there is no risk of dangerous solvent residues. Using high pressure and temperature, carbon dioxide molecules alternate between liquid and solid forms. This is called the supercritical phase. In the liquid form, the carbon dioxide dissolves the oleoresin molecules, which solidify during the solid phase. Supercritical fluid extraction is costly and has not been widely adopted in the oleoresin industry. However, a number of producers who use the technology label their products as organic. SCF research using small mounts of a co-solvent such as ethanol (beverage alcohol) or enzymes shows promise.

Uses of Pepper 7

ORLD DEMAND FOR PEPPER is growing. In this chapter, how pepper is used and what it is used for will shed some more light on the demand side of the pepper industry. Some of this increased demand for pepper as a seasoning is due to population growth and improvement in income in populous countries such as China. Simultaneously, per capita use is increasing, related to the popularity of processed food products. Other uses of pepper are also on the rise. Pepper is an effective preservative, antioxidant, and antimicrobial additive to food, with no allergic or physical side effects. Pepper has a long history as medicinal ingredient. More recently, research is uncovering properties of piperine that affect the efficacy with which many drugs are absorbed by the body. Piperine is used in emollient skin creams and is an effective insect repellent. The essential oils obtained from pepper are a component of many popular perfumes.

Culinary Uses of Pepper

The use of spices varies greatly depending on the culture and region of the world. Kenji Hirasa and Mitsui Takamasa,[1] two Japanese spice researchers, proposed a patterning theory of spice use that measures the utilization of a spice with locally produced foods as a synthesis of palatability that occurs in the mouth. By analyzing recipes, they painstakingly mapped the utility of spices by region and culture. They created "spice maps" consisting of radians projecting outward from a central point, something like the hands on a clock. There are radians for French, Italian, German, British, American, Southeast Asian, Chinese, and Japanese cuisines. The radians were organized around the central point, with Eastern cooking cultures on the left side and Western cooking on the right side. The length of each radian was determined by counting the number of times a spice is used in local recipes and expressing it as a percentage of the total number of recipes examined. The radian projects farther out from the center as the percentage of use in regional recipes increases. A shape created by joining the ends of the radians is the "map" or pattern. A circular pattern means the spice is used uniformly across all cuisines in the analysis. If the shape is cockeyed, then one group of cuisines uses the spice more (or less) than others. In all, separate maps for each of forty different food-flavoring ingredients (most of which were spices) were developed. The shape for pepper was close to a circle, with a dimple for Japan (where the least pepper is used) and a bulge for the United States (where most pepper is used). With the exception of garlic and onion (arguably food items rather than spices), pepper was the most universally employed spice in the world. Pepper is truly the world's favorite spice across cultures, not just in terms of volume.

The taste and aroma of pepper is best when freshly ground on top of the food just before eating. The use of pepper as a condiment is a ritual act for many people who people habitually sprinkle or grind a few particles of pepper on their food without much thought. A condiment is defined as a flavoring mixture added to foods when eaten (not during cooking). In many cases, people are not fully aware of the contribution to taste and aroma that is taking place. Small amounts of pre-ground pepper found in pepper shakers that have languished at the table for many months (or even years) will have a minor effect on taste and even less on aroma because a large proportion of the chavicine will have morphed into piperine. The volatile aromatic components will have disappeared into the environment long ago. The lack of contribution to taste may be due to using an insufficient quantity. Partially clogged pepper shakers in restaurants and homes are more common than not. Thankfully, servers in better restaurants bring the pepper mill to the table and offer a fresh grind to top off your meal.

Why is pepper so much better when used as a condiment? Although black pepper contains an average of 10 percent piperine by weight, only a single gram of piperine will dissolve in twenty-five liters of water at room temperature (20°C). Notwithstanding that six times that much (six grams in twenty-five liters) will dissolve in boiling water, it is still a very tiny amount, almost undetectable in the mouth. You can demonstrate this at home. Put a tablespoon of fresh peppercorns into a cup (250 ml), and add boiling water as if you were making tea. Even after steeping for several minutes, very little pungency is imparted to the water despite the very substantial amount of pepper used. Water in food does not readily absorb the taste of pepper. Tiny flakes of pepper, freshly ground on the food just before eating are a much better way to get the aroma and taste. If you are in the mood to do a few more experiments, try these. Find four clean, small (200 ml or less) jars with lids. Put a teaspoon of peppercorns into each jar. Add water, vinegar, oil, and vodka to each jar in turn, then put on the lids and label them. After a week or so, taste the liquid from the middle (below the surface) in each of the jars using a straw. A small amount of piperine can float to the top in the water and vinegar jars. Peppercorns soaking in every jar will impart a dark color from nonaromatic or pungent compounds. These dark-colored compounds do not taste or smell like pepper.

It should be no surprise that the water does not take on a pungent taste or aroma. This is because the piperine and essential oils do not dissolve in water to any meaningful extent. Peppercorns soaked in vinegar are similar, although you may get a little pungency if you can get past the sour taste and pickle-like smell. Vinegar is about 5 percent acetic acid. Only highly concentrated acetic acid can absorb piperine, and even then, it is a relatively small amount. It makes you wonder about the role peppercorns play in pickling spice mixtures.

Piperine is extremely soluble in alcohol: one gram in fifteen milliliters. That is 1,600 times as much as the solubility in water. Even though vodka is only 40 percent alcohol by volume (the rest is water), it has a very pungent taste and aroma. After your experimentation is done, use can use your pepper-infused vodka to make a Bloody Mary. Piperine is highly soluble in oil. After a week, the oil is distinctly pungent and aromatic. Doing the same experiment with whole milk gives a far more pungent result than water or vinegar because the milk fat readily absorbs piperine. Try the recipe for Thandai in chapter 9. Dairy fats in particular seem to complement pepper very well. Crush a tablespoon of peppercorns in a mortar and pestle and fry them in a pan with some butter for a few seconds. The aroma is spectacular, and the piperine-infused butter easily transfers the flavor to any food that is prepared using it. The taste and aroma of pepper is highlighted in dishes such as steak au poivre, cognac pepper sauce, and Singaporean black pepper crab (not to be confused with chili crab), where the aroma and taste have been absorbed into a lipid (fat) base. Pepper flavor and aroma can be infused into olive oil by soaking a few peppercorns in oil for several weeks. Peppercorns can be pounded with cold, unsalted butter to be used as a finish for grilled meats, seafood, or vegetables, imparting both aroma and flavor. Peppercorns placed on the fat side of a steak or roast infuse the pepper taste well into the meat as the fat continuously bastes the food during cooking. Pepper readily flavors cheese. These techniques work by absorbing aroma and taste into lipids: any kind of fat works well.

Many spices are added to food while it is being cooked. Absorption of the pepper depends entirely on the fat content of the food; however, as foods cook, the pepper aroma decreases. The essential oils and aromatic components of pepper are volatile. Even when captured by fats or by mixing into a semi-solid such as a purée or gravy, the aroma disperses into the atmosphere when heated. This is why most chefs adjust the seasoning of dishes (tempering) just prior to serving. Tempering provides the best possible aroma and taste. It is also why pepper (along with salt) is the only seasoning commonly made available at the table.

Gravies, thickened soups, and sauces suspend the freshly ground pepper without dissolving it. Grinding fresh peppercorns at the time of use is the best way to add black pepper to a dish. Particularly in foods containing little or no fats, direct ingestion of the ground or crushed peppercorns by sprinkling is the most efficient way to deliver the aroma and taste. Use the grinder close to the food. Ground pepper can easily irritate the mucous membranes in the nose. Sneezing (called sternutation) is how the body tries to expel the pepper dust and is a sure way to spoil a great dinner.

As much as 48 percent of pepper is distributed already ground for the sake of convenience. Sophisticated buyers such as food processors and chefs (who do not have time to hand grind peppercorns) will often specify the size of the "grind" depending on its intended use. The size of the grind is measured by mesh size. A mesh is simply a metal sheet with holes in it or a screen woven from wire. The larger the mesh size number, the finer the grind. A mesh will prevent larger particles from passing through, but not smaller ones. The best whole Tellicherry peppercorns (greater than 4.25 mm) would pass through mesh size 4, but not mesh size 5. Half or quarter-cracked pepper (mesh sizes 6–10) is used for pepper-encrusted dishes. Coarse ground (mesh sizes 12–14) pepper is used on roasted chickens, steaks, burgers, and other meats that do not have a fat cap. Ground pepper that will be used in pepper shakers at the table needs to be more finely ground (18–28 mesh) in order to pass through the small holes in the top of the shaker. Finely ground pepper (30–34 mesh) is used in brown sauces because it is less visible. Ground white pepper (60 mesh) is used in mashed potatoes or white sauces, where it is virtually invisible.

Other considerations for specifying the mesh size is spice blending. When producing spice blends, it is important that the mesh sizes of all components are similar; otherwise, the smaller particles will migrate and settle on the bottom of the container. This can alter the composition of the seasoning mix as it used. The bigger particles will be dispensed first, followed by smaller particles as the container is emptied. Next time you buy a spice blend, look at the bottom of the container. If a lot of "dust" has settled there, you may wish to choose another manufacturer, or at least mix it up thoroughly before using.

Pepper is often used in combination with salt. Pepper increases the perceived salty taste of foods. If very little salt is used, pepper will decrease the salty sensation by overpowering it. However, if a moderate amount of salt is used, for example, a cup of bouillon, it will taste more salty if pepper is added. Researchers have found that medium-ground pepper delivers a stronger taste than fine-ground pepper. The perceived saltiness in the presence of pepper increases more as the actual salt concentration increases.[2] The taste of pepper is not sweet, sour, salty, bitter, or savory. Thus, it can is used to complement any tastes or taste combinations. Countless dishes marry the taste and aroma of black pepper with other flavoring agents; for example, seafood seasoned with lemon and pepper, cured meats such as salami and capocollo, cheeses, pepper-encrusted red meats, pepper-topped pâtés, cracked pepper crackers, strawberry-pepper tarts, chocolate pepper steak rub, and pfeffernusse cookies. Pepper plays an integral role in curry powder, garam masala, pickling spice, *quatre épices* (pepper, cloves, nutmeg, and ginger), and Chinese five-spice powder.

There is agreement among pepper aficionados that there is variety in the flavor (both taste and smell) of pepper produced in different parts of the world, and even from different growers. There is much less agreement between individual tasters. One must keep in mind that evaluating the flavor of complex items is at best an inexact science. The method used to evaluate the organoleptic properties of pepper varies also. One method is simply to put a small amount of freshly ground pepper on the tongue and savor it. Breathing out through the nose (retronasal) will trigger the aroma response. However, one must be prepared for the inevitable sneezing, watery eyes, and irritation that may follow. Doing comparisons by this method is difficult because the senses are easily overwhelmed, and may take some time to recover between samples.

A better method is to evaluate pepper in the context of a neutral backdrop that has no discernible aroma or taste. A portion of plain, cold, unsalted boiled rice is sprinkled with freshly ground pepper and placed in a plastic bag then massaged and squeezed with the hands for a minute or two until it has warmed. The bag is then opened and the aroma is sniffed. Tasting of the rice follows. This has the advantage of not overwhelming the palate, evaluating aroma and taste independently as well as together. Some tasters will use plain, cold mashed potatoes in a similar manner, refreshing the palate with unsalted soda crackers between pepper samples. *America's Test Kitchen* (a popular television show in North America) tested several kinds of Tellicherry pepper directly on the tongue, and then in a more applied context by using it on foods where pepper is often used, such as scrambled eggs, tomato soup, and pepper-encrusted steaks. Since no one actually eats pepper in isolation, there is a certain appeal to trying it on foods where it is commonly used. Curiously, the testers found differences in the pepper taken directly on the tongue, but to a much lesser degree when sprinkled on foods.

Regardless of how you perform the organoleptic evaluation of pepper, there are a number of relatively common terms used to describe pepper. Among these are *fruity, floral, musty, astringent, warm, soft, biting, cardboard, resinous, floral, bitter, cedar,* and *menthol.* Some tasters use terms including *lemon zest, lime, camphor, eucalyptus,* and even *carbolic soap!* In short, descriptions are as creative as those who utter them, and differences are less notable in the foods seasoned with the pepper.

Pepper as a Food Preservative

Common folklore says that pepper was used to cover the taste of rotting meat. Nothing could be further from the truth. In medieval Europe, black pepper was worth as much as gold, and only the well-off, powerful members of society could afford to buy it. Meat was readily available on a year-round basis through farming and hunting activities and was inexpensive by comparison. Meat was consumed fresh within a short time after the animal was killed. The knowledge needed to preserve meats by salting, drying, smoking, curing, or pickling was widespread. Why would anyone waste extremely valuable pepper on meat that had gone bad? Sailors and soldiers on long campaigns such as those in the Napoleonic wars would rarely, if ever, eat tainted meat. On land, soldiers could not march into battle effectively if they were suffering from food poisoning. Foot soldiers, artillery, and cavalry would buy or commandeer fresh supplies locally as they were required. Sailors could not operate the ships that were heavily reliant on robust human labor if they were ill with food poisoning. Live poultry, goats, sheep, cows, and pigs were carried on board to supply milk, eggs, and ultimately, meat. From time to time, rations were supplemented at sea by catching fish, marine mammals, turtles, or sea birds.[3] Under the watchful care of a quartermaster, preserved meats brought along on these campaigns were issued and used up well before turning bad.

However, rather than cover the taste of rotting meat, the essential oil of pepper (piperine) has properties that can extend the storage life of many food products. Two important factors in preserving food are suppression of microbial growth and oxidation. Many people prefer natural preservatives to chemical agents such as sulfites; consequently, there has been considerable scientific interest in the antimicrobial properties of black pepper. A substantial body of research over the past twenty years confirms the effectiveness of pepper as a food preservative. A paper published by the Council of Scientific and Industrial Research by Karsha and Lakshmi[4] in 2010 concluded that black pepper provides excellent inhibition of the growth of bacteria such as *Staphylococcus aureus, Bacillus cereus, Streptococcus faecalis, Pseudomonas aeruginosa, Salmonella typhi,* and *Escherichia coli.* Staph bacteria cause skin infections, abscesses, respiratory infections (such as sinusitis), and food poisoning. *Bacillus cereus* is a fast-growing bacterium that can cause nausea, vomiting, and diarrhea. *Pseudomonas aeruginosa* is a multi-drug-resistant, opportunistic bacterium that usually appears after infection by another virus or bacterium. It can cause inflammation of organs and sepsis. Salmonella, a common cause of food poisoning, can also lead to typhoid fever. *E-coli* is well known for food poisoning and the recall of ground beef products. All of these potentially nasty pathogens are common. Particularly in prepared meats, pâtés, and aspics that provide ideal growing mediums for bacteria, pepper makes these items safer to eat. Using levels of essential oil in concentrations similar to those found in many prepared food products, the authors of another study[5] found that both green and black pepper oils significantly reduced the growth of fifteen food spoilage microorganisms found in food, including several pathogenic molds.

Aside from spoilage and food safety issues, the quality of preserved foods is affected by oxidation. When compounds found in food are exposed to oxygen, their composition changes and they begin to break down. Oxidized fats taste rancid and stale. Pigments in red meat change to a gray color. Vitamins lose their potency. Oxidation does not make food unsafe; it makes it unpalatable. Wrapping foods in a barrier film (such as Saran wrap) prevents oxidation by isolating the food from the air. Other means of preventing oxidation are chemical in nature. For example, sulfites combine with oxygen more readily than the compounds found in food, with the result that the foods containing sulfites are protected from oxidation. Researchers have found that certain spices are highly effective antioxidants in concentrations similar to those used in food preparation. Pepper was the third-most-effective antioxidant after cloves and cinnamon.[6]

Medical Uses of Pepper

Alternative medical practice is growing in popularity in many countries. Sometimes it offers hope where modern medical practice has failed to provide solutions. For the world's poor, it is often the only affordable treatment option. Alternative medicine is an alternative to modern medicine because it offers "natural" therapies that are unproven using modern scientific methods. Responding to accusations of quackery, the alternative medical industry (worth $5 billion in the United States) has repositioned itself as complementary or integrative medicine. Proponents of alternative medicine often claim that drug companies who want to sell their medicines will not go to the expense of testing low-cost herbs and supplements. Whether or not you believe in alternative medicine, much of the early knowledge concerning the use of pepper as a medical therapy was developed based on repeated observations and trial and error. Shamans, healers, and others formulated pseudoscientific theories to explain how and why things worked. Observation was the scientific methodology of the day, and although it lacked the technology and rigor of the modern scientific method, useful knowledge was gained. The efficacy of some of these ancient practices is being investigated using modern scientific research methods.

Ayurveda, also known as traditional Indian medicine, has been practiced for three thousand years, and by some estimates, 80 percent of India's population still uses it exclusively or in conjunction with modern medicine. The Indian government began to regulate and standardize Ayurvedic medical practice in 1970. Today, more than one hundred eighty educational institutions offer degrees in Ayurvedic medicine. Western societies recognize Ayurveda as one of several alternative medical practices, including TCM (Traditional Chinese Medicine), homeopathy, naturopathy, chiropractic, and acupuncture, among others.

The pseudoscientific theory of Ayurveda espouses that the body is comprised of three doshas, or elemental states (Vata, Pitta, and Kapha) that must be in balance in order to have good health. Treatments to restore balance to the doshas typically involve plant-based medicines, nutrition, purification, massage, exercise (yoga), meditation, and some (increasingly rare) surgical procedures. Practitioners of Ayurveda believe pepper enhances digestion, elimination, and circulation; reduces flatulence; stimulates the appetite; and maintains respiratory system and joint health. It clearly stimulates appetite by making bland foods taste and smell delicious! The vast majority of Ayurvedic preparations consist of complex combinations of items. Pepper is most often used as a component of the *trikatu* (three pungents) consisting of *Piper nigrum*, *Piper longam*, and *Zingiber officinale* (ginger). The trikatu are an important part of many Ayurvedic formulations. Consistent with Ayurvedic practice, pepper was a cure-all during Roman times, much like aspirin is today. It was an easy medicine to prescribe: pepper was readily available, and a popular food spice, too.

Uses of pepper within the TCM framework are similar to those of Ayurvedic practice. This is not coincidental, because from the fourth through eighth centuries, written Ayurvedic medical texts were translated into Chinese. Ancient Indian medical texts, such as Ashtangahridaya and Samhitas, prescribe the use of pepper in complex medical formulations consisting of many ingredients. Along with pepper from the Malabar Coast, Ayurveda became widely adopted and was incorporated into TCM. In addition to digestive tract and circulatory issues, TCM uses pepper to treat brain function maladies, for example epilepsy.

Modern versions of alternative medical practice involving the medicinal use of pepper is primarily in the domain of naturopathy, homeopathy, and aromatherapy. Claims by practitioners of these popular alternative medical practices include health benefits of black pepper with weight loss, skin health, digestion, dental caries, and inflammation.

Scientific Research on Medical Uses of Black Pepper

After they are scientifically proven, alternative medical treatments become part of modern medical practice. One of the most important and promising research developments is the use of piperine as a bioavailability enhancer. Bioprene (trade name BioPerine) is a highly purified and standardized extract of pepper containing 95 percent piperine. Bioprene has been approved by the FDA as a bioavailability enhancer. Bioavailability refers to how much of the main pharmacological ingredient in a drug is absorbed into the body. Drugs can be administered orally, intravenously, by inhalation through the lungs, or absorption by tissues such as the skin (the patch), nose (snorting), and rectum (plugging). There is a reason why street drug users administer drugs by injection into veins. If the same drug were ingested, much less would enter the bloodstream. Our digestive systems are particularly good at metabolizing or preventing the absorption of certain drugs. In some cases, more than 98 percent of an orally administered drug is not absorbed into the bloodstream. For example, alendronic acid (sold under the trade name Fosamax) used in the treatment of osteoporosis has as little as 0.6–0.7 percent bioavailability.

This is the bioavailability problem. Drug development involves the integration of a newly discovered pharmacological molecule with the development of a formulation that maximizes the amount of the drug that actually enters the bloodstream. It is not as simple as increasing the amount of the medicine to compensate for low bioavailability. Not all components of a drug have the same bioavailability. While generic drugs are often comparable to brand-name drugs, significant debate continues surrounding the bioavailability of generic drugs that reach the site of action.[7] Piperine has the ability to improve the pharmacological efficiency of many drugs by affecting the bioavailability: the amount of a drug that enters the circulation system. Studies have shown that piperine can increase the absorption of anti-epileptic medications (phenytoin), blood pressure medications (propanolol), tuberculosis drugs (rifampicin), painkillers (diclofenac), and some anticancer drugs.[8]

The benefits of piperine go beyond bioavailability. In a review of research about the pharmacological potential of pepper,[9] the authors found published evidence that piperine has antimicrobial, antioxidant, anticancer, anti-inflammatory, antidepressant, anti-diarrheal, anticonvulsant, and analgesic properties. Most of this research was carried out on small animals (mice and hamsters) and should not be taken as strong evidence of piperine's effectiveness in humans. Piperine increases the rate of metabolite conversion (conversion of food into compounds that are metabolized by the body). It slows down the activity of enzymes that break down drugs already in the system, allowing them to remain effective longer with smaller, less frequent doses. Ongoing animal studies are providing encouraging results.

Alzheimer's disease is caused by a buildup of amyloidal plaque formation in the arteries of the brain. The FDA has approved cholinesterase inhibitors for the treatment of memory loss in Alzheimer's patients. Early-stage research using animal models show that piperine was effective in reducing the level of cholinesterase by 26 percent.[10] More recent research in 2016 confirms this result.[11]

Some research using human subjects has taken place. Dr. Jed E. Rose, best known as the coinventor of the nicotine patch, published results from a study with coauthor F. M. Behm that demonstrated that black pepper oil administered via a substitute cigarette device reduced cigarette cravings and could be useful in smoking-cessation programs.[12]

Difficulty in swallowing is called dysphagia. Patients who suffer extreme dysphagia are unable to swallow solids without difficulty. This makes eating solid food and taking pills very difficult and potentially hazardous if the airway becomes blocked (choking). Patients who suffer from dysphagia are given thickened liquids (Thick-it or Thicken-up) to make swallowing easier. A study published in the *Journal of Gastroenterology* in 2014 found that supplementing a food bolus (morsel) or pill with piperine speeds swallowing and strongly improves safety.[13]

Researchers at Dalhousie University (Halifax, Canada) found evidence that piperine was effective in the treatment of colon cancer by inhibiting cancerous cell growth and increasing aptoptosis, the normal programmed death of cells.[14] Recent research also has found that piperine helps prevent mutation of methicillin-resistant *Staphlococcus aureus* (MRSA) bacteria when administered with Ciprofloxacin, an antibiotic used to treat a wide variety of antibiotic-resistant bacteria.[15]

The aromatic components of pepper do not come from piperine (which adds pungency to taste). They come from the essential oil of pepper, extracted from pepper oleoresin. Chemists have identified the major compounds that are the source of pepper's complex, alluring aroma. Aromatic components of the essential oil of pepper include lilac (α-terpineol), vanilla (piperonal), green apple (hexanol), fresh-herbal-spicy (nerol and nerolidol), camphor-eucalyptus (1, 8-cineol), woody (dihydrocarveol), citrus (citral), and pine (α-Pinene) along with a spicy, sharp, irritating aroma (acetophenone). Some of these aromatic components have medicinal qualities, although they are not extracted from the essential oil of pepper for these purposes. For example, α-Pinene is a bronchodilator with high (60 percent) bioavailability that is useful in the treatment of asthma. Piperonal (also called heliotropin) can be used in the synthesis of tadalafil (Cialis) and astrasentan, an experimental anti-small-cell lung cancer drug. Nerolidol is known to have antioxidant, anticancer and antimicrobial properties.

Use as a Fragrance

The essential oil of pepper recently has had a revival in perfumery. The volatile essential oils extracted from pepper provide a bright accent top note in fragrances (particularly men's cologne). The spicy-aromatic and musky men's perfume Harmony AXE uses as much as 6 percent pepper oil. Other well-known perfume brands include Aramis for Men, Strictly Night (Jil Sander), Terre de Hermes, Fierce Icon (Abercrombie and Fitch), and Extreme Polo Sport (Ralph Lauren), among many others.

Pepper as an Insect Repellent

Picaridin (also known as icaridine), a derivative of piperine, is used in some insect repellent products such as the OFF! Family Care brand. Studies have shown picaridin to be as effective as DEET in repelling mosquitoes. The Public Health Agency of Canada's Canadian Advisory Committee on Tropical Medicine and Travel names icaridine as the first-choice repellent for children under twelve years of age. Picaridin is odorless, non-greasy, and does not dissolve plastics or other synthetics.

Piperine can also be used as an effective, natural insecticide for control of tent caterpillars and saw worm in trees and shrubs.[16] Due to its cost, while piperine may be useful, it is not necessarily cost effective.

Buying Pepper

8

THIS CHAPTER DEALS WITH QUALITY ISSUES that affect pepper and the efforts of regulatory bodies and spice traders to maximize the safety, purity, and quality of the pepper we use. The efforts of regulators and spice merchants are reassuring: the vast proportion of the pepper we consume is wholesome and safe. Buying pepper for personal use is quite different from buying pepper as an importer for subsequent resale to consumers, commercial processors, and packagers. Individuals can purchase small amounts of pepper for their own use from international vendors on the internet. Small amounts pass border and customs inspection without any fuss, and often no import duty is charged. The situation for importers who use or resell pepper is quite different. Food and drug acts in every country regulate the importation and sale of most food products in the interest of public safety and environmental security. Although spices in general are considered to have a low public health risk, imported pepper is subject to inspection, testing, and certification.

Safety

Most people do not associate pepper with food safety or food security issues. Perhaps the following examples will change your mind. On January 23, 2010, a well-known US producer of Italian-style meats, Daniele International, voluntarily withdrew 1,240,000 pounds of their products under a Class 1 recall. Class 1 recalls are for defective products that can cause serious illness or death. The meats were contaminated with *Salmonella montevideo* and *Salmonella senftenberg* bacteria strains. Along with eighty other salmonella bacterium strains, *Salmonella montevideo* and *Salmonella senftenberg* can make people very sick, sometimes resulting in death. The Centers for Disease Control in Atlanta confirmed that 272 people in forty-four states who had consumed the affected Daniele products had become ill with the bacteria. The source of the contamination was traced to black pepper and crushed red pepper purchased from two different American suppliers that had obtained the spices from Vietnamese sources. Somehow, the contaminated shipments had passed through the regulatory inspection process when they were imported.

In 2013, nine hundred tons of pepper were seized along with four hundred liters of mineral oil and paraffin (kerosene) from a spice warehouse in Chennai, India.[1] Old, dry-looking peppercorns had been tumbled in a cement mixer with small amounts of mineral oil to give them a rich, dark luster and thus a higher price when sold. Mineral oil used in adulterated black pepper is a mixture of burned diesel, paraffin, naphta, and other petroleum products. Black pepper coated with mineral oil is unfit for human consumption and potentially carcinogenic. The Food Safety and Standards Authority of India (FSSAI) estimated that 10 percent of the pepper held in the National Commodity and Derivatives Exchange (NCDEX) warehouses was contaminated with oil. One of the issues Indian spice traders have with the new commodity exchanges that replaced the old Pepper Exchange in Cochin is that the quality of the pepper being traded is not assured, as it once was when traders knew each other and developed relationships based on trust. The FSSAI impounded the oiled pepper and ordered it destroyed.

These two examples of contamination in the pepper supply chain are extreme. There are literally hundreds of recalls involving contaminated pepper, although most are smaller quantities. They illustrate the challenge faced, on one hand, by governments of importing countries to protect consumers from potentially harmful pepper and, on the other, the governments of exporting countries to protect markets for producers.

Ensuring food safety is the mandate of regulatory bodies in virtually every country in the world. The World Trade Organization (WTO) consists of 164 members representing the world's countries in matters of trade, including food products. National regulatory bodies exist in virtually every importing country in the world. In North America, the Food and Drug Administration (FDA), US Department of Agriculture (USDA), and the Canadian Food Inspection Agency (CFIA) are responsible for the importation of food products. The Food Safety and Standards Authority of India (FSSAI) is a regulatory body that certifies export shipments before they leave India. Commercial spice exporters, processors, and marketing companies are committed to providing high-quality, safe products to their international customers. They have a shared interest in making sure the products they handle pass through the regulatory system efficiently so they may conduct their business without recalls and the interruption of the supply system due to impounded or condemned shipments.

Many international and spice trading associations have been established to work with national regulators. By working together, standards, certification, and remediation procedures can expedite transactions to everyone's benefit. The bewildering number of international, national, and commercial spice trade associations reflects the magnitude of the world's spice trade.

The International Organization of Spice Trade Associations (IOSTA) is an umbrella group that incorporates representatives from spice trading organizations around the world. Its members include the All Nippon Spice Association (ANSA), American Spice Trade Association (ASTA), Australian Food and Grocery Council (AFGC), Canadian Spice Association (CSA), Department of Export Agriculture in Sri Lanka (DEA), European Spice Association (ESA), International General Produce Association (IGPA), Spice Council of Sri Lanka, Spices Board of India, and the Vietnamese Pepper Association (VPA). It is interesting to note that the IGPA, based in London, traces its roots all the way back to the Pepperer's Guild (1180 CE) and the Company of Merchant Adventurers (forerunner of the British East India Company) formed in 1599 CE.

Merchant groups have also organized to advocate for policy and regulation of the spice industry. National Seasoning Manufacturers Association (NSMA), World Spice Association (Cochin, India), Seasoning and Spice Association (SSA, UK) are a few examples. Many spice industry players belong to multiple organizations. One only has to visit the websites of any of these organizations to see that food safety and security regulations are high-ranking concerns as reflected in policy statements, subcommittees, and meeting agendas. Pepper, the most traded spice in the world, figures highly in the business and discussions.

Prior to 2011, the FDA's mission was to detect contaminated pepper and respond to contamination with recalls. At one point, the bacterial contamination-testing problem was massive. The FDA had limited preventive potential and a very small proportion of imported products were tested. It simply was not possible for the FDA to test every shipment of pepper entering the United States. Consequently, a program of random sampling, followed by testing of the samples, was in place. The results of the random sampling program revealed that a significant amount of the imported pepper was contaminated. From December 1, 1986, through

May 31, 1987, inspectors rejected one-third of sampled shipments. To address this problem, an agreement in 1988 with the Export Inspection Council of the Indian Ministry of Commerce required them to test and certify every shipment of pepper to the United States. The program was successful: none of the certified shipments were rejected by FDA quality audits in the following year. Most other countries did not have such an agreement in place.

This and other issues led to the passage of the Food Safety Modernization Act, signed into law by President Obama in 2011. The Food Safety Modernization Act shifted the responsibility for food safety from the FDA to the importers. One of the key features of the new approach is the Foreign Supplier Verification Program,[2] which requires that food importers verify that their imports meet US standards. There are a number of exemptions or modified compliance rules. Among the exemptions are small quantities for research, evaluation, or personal use, and the importation of specific foods from countries that have a recognized food-safety system equivalent to that of the United States. It seems that many hands make light work, at least for the FDA. The full implementation date for the Foreign Supplier Verification Program was May 30, 2017.

As of 2015, food importers could use an accredited third party to verify that their imported food shipments meet US safety standards. Third-party agencies can be companies (private or corporate) or government bodies in pepper-exporting countries. The accredited third-party agencies test and issue certificates of compliance for all food product shipments imported into the United States, much like the Indian Export Inspection Council did in 1988. The FDA developed a procedure for third-party agencies to apply for accreditation, subject to meeting a series of stringent requirements. The FDA audits the certificates issued by each third-party agency to ensure they are doing their job meticulously. The benefits of the FSVP are clear: all shipments are checked, the cost of testing is born by the importer, and the supply chain flows smoothly. A second feature of the program allows remedial processing of pepper shipments after they have entered the United States. This enables importers to import pepper that will be brought into compliance after it has arrived in the United States.

Most of the spice industry organizations have developed documents that describe standards and procedures for spice production, processing, and trading. Salmonella contamination and oiled pepper is not the only problem consumers may face when buying pepper. Chemical residues, feces, rodent hair, dust, and dirt are common contaminants of pepper. Adulteration of pepper by mixing in papaya seeds also takes place. The problem of contamination and quality assurance is as old as the pepper trade itself. Garbling, the practice of cleaning and ensuring the quality of pepper, became a standard operating procedure of the Pepperer's Guild of London, founded in 1180 to defend consumers against unscrupulous spice traders.

Contaminated pepper begins at the source: third world countries located in the equatorial zones of the world. Standards of cleanliness, food handling, and storage in the third world are very different compared to those practiced by consumers in developed countries in Europe, North America, Australia, and Japan. A great deal of the disease and hardship experienced by the poor people who live in the producing countries can be attributed to poor sanitation, dirty water, and food-quality issues. Outright starvation or lack of food is a much less common problem than contaminated food and impure water. The poor are subject to many diseases and ills associated with a lack of proper sanitation, wholesome food, and potable water. They are often the same people that work in the cultivation, harvesting, and processing of spice crops. In many cases, it is not a lack of care or attention by hardworking growers; it is a lack of knowledge and training. Unwittingly, some of their own problems with disease caused by filth are exported along with the spices.

Many disease-causing pathogens and foreign matter are introduced to spices during fertilizer application, harvesting, processing, and storage before finding their way to consumers in the West. The opportunities for contamination begin with failure to adhere to good agricultural practices. Most contaminants are introduced to the peppercorns at the farm site. Microbial contamination primarily consists of *Salmonella*; however, *Bacillus cereus*, *Clostridium perfringens*, *Cronobacter spp.*, *Shigella*, and *Staphylococcus aureus* (all of which are common causes of food poisoning) have also been identified. The *Salmonella* bacterium can survive for a year on dry peppercorns, and much longer in the case of ground pepper. *Salmonella* populations can increase on peppercorns that are not fully dried, or during humid, hot storage conditions.

Salmonella is introduced to the farm site by an animal host and can persist in the environment for several years. Wild birds, chickens, farm animals used for plowing, or just animals foraging for food are all potential sources of salmonella contamination on the farm. Proactive spice companies that have contracts with growers deliver training programs developed by the World Health Organization (Codex Alimentarius[3]) limiting animals in the growing area, the use of unclean irrigation water, farmer hygiene, manuring, harvesting, drying, and storage practices. Most of the recommended procedures are common sense and simple to perform.

Growers should provide sanitary toilet facilities for workers and hand-washing stations during harvest and drying times. Animal manure must be treated (well composted and solarized) before application and should be applied no later than three months before harvest. Harvest containers should be clean and sanitized before using. Drying should take place on clean concrete, tile, or plastic, never on bare ground. Covers should be rigged over the drying pepper to prevent contamination by bird droppings. Mechanical drying is preferred to sun drying. Pepper must be packed in new, unused bags for transport. These simple techniques go a long way to reducing biological contaminants.

In addition to bacterial agents, mycotoxins may also be present in peppercorns or ground pepper. Aflatoxin and ochratoxin are dangerous toxins (called metabolites) produced by strains of *Aspergillus flavus*, *Aspergillus ochrceus*, and *Aspergillus alliaceus*. These toxin-producing fungi are found in soils around the world and occur naturally in the environment where pepper is grown. Aflatoxin and ochratoxin are among the most powerful carcinogens known to man, even in minute quantities. The USDA specifies that foods must contain less than twenty parts per billion of aflatoxin to be safe. The EU standard is even less (5 ppb). Keeping molds under control in the field goes a long way toward minimizing their presence in the pepper berries. Mycotoxin levels in pepper are elevated by improper processing and storage. Surface cleaning alone is ineffective in inhibiting growth of the fungi inside the peppercorn. Spores can grow inside the peppercorn if it is not dried quickly and thoroughly to 11 percent moisture or less. Peppercorns stored in humid environments reabsorb moisture that supports the growth of fungi and production of the toxins. The presence of mycotoxins in ground pepper tends to be higher than in whole peppercorns. Mycotoxins are a major concern in oleoresins because the production process concentrates mycotoxins.

The US Food and Drug Administration produced an extensive document in 2013 that identifies many contamination and adulteration issues among spices imported into the United States.[4] The easiest kind of contamination to detect is contamination by extraneous materials (the technical description is *filth*). Filth includes insects (live and dead, whole, parts, or eggs), feces (human, animal, bird, and insect), hair (human, rodent, bat, cow, sheep, dog, cat, and others), and materials such as decomposed matter and bird feather fragments. From time to time stones, twigs, synthetic fibers, and even rubber bands are found in pepper shipments.

Most of the filth is insect fragments and animal hair, indicating poor or inadequate storage and packing conditions. Aggregators (local traders) typically heap the peppercorns on a concrete floor, trusting feral cats in the neighborhood to keep the rodent population at bay! When enough pepper has been accumulated, it is shoveled into bags along with sweepings: not the most sanitary food handling practice. Fortunately, pepper sold in this way will be garbled further down the supply chain before it is exported.

Garbling is the name of the process used to clean and grade the peppercorns. Exporters must garble the peppercorns until no filth contaminants are visible to the eye before being shipped. Filth is removed by garbling machines, although no single machine can adequately clean pepper on its own. In simple systems (primarily used by exporters), the first stage is to remove dust by aspirating (vacuuming) the peppercorns as they fall through an upward-moving air column inside a vertical tunnel. As the peppercorns fall downward, the dust is swept upward and out of the tunnel by the moving air. In the second stage, a vibrating horizontal surface with screens of various sizes separate peppercorns from debris and sort them by size. A better, more sophisticated system is a machine called a gravity separator. A vibrating horizontal surface (similar to a tabletop) perforated with thousands of tiny holes is slightly tilted on two axes, lengthwise and sideways. Peppercorns are introduced to the upper edge of the surface. Air

Photo 8.1.   Black peppercorns ready for garbling. J. Barth (Author)

blows through the perforated surface from below, "fluidizing" the pepper-corns. Heavier particles "float" toward the lower side and bottom of the tilted surface by gravity. Lighter particles move to the top. Somewhere in between, the cleaned and sorted peppercorns are located and withdrawn. Gravity separating machines are able to remove filth of all kinds (particularly small stones) and sort the pepper by size at the same time.

Spiral (cyclone) separators have largely superseded gravity separators. Cyclone separators work by introducing the peppercorns tangentially into the top of a vertically oriented, cone-shaped chamber using compressed air. The peppercorns, propelled by the compressed air, spin around with increasing rapidity as they fall downward toward the narrow bottom of the cone. Lighter-weight impurities are drawn out from the center of the cyclone chamber by a vacuum applied to a tube near the top. By varying the air pressure and the speed at which the peppercorns go around in the chamber, different sizes of particles are withdrawn from the separator. Light berries (peppercorns with an undeveloped seed inside) can also be removed using this device.

Other machines are able to separate whiteheads (peppercorns that have lost their pericarp) from black pepper corns using optical detectors and little jets of air to blow away the undesirable peppercorns. Ferrous metal fragments (usually originating from damaged or poorly maintained machinery) are removed by passing the pepper over strong magnets. The presence of non-ferrous metal fragments are detected with metal detectors. Garbling is important for spice manufacturers: debris (such as stones or metal fragments) can damage expensive grinding and packaging equipment.

Whole-pepper shipments with more than 1 percent by weight of moldy, insect-infested peppercorns, or foreign matter, or more than one milligram per pound of mammalian excreta (dung) are rejected or reprocessed. The criteria for ground pepper are similar. If six or more fifty-gram samples taken from a ground pepper shipment contain more than 475 insect fragments, the entire shipment is unfit for use as food and rejected. If more than one rodent hair fragment per fifty-gram sample is found, the shipment is rejected.

A second development in the process for importing pepper under the new rules was the opportunity for importers to perform remedial processing in the United States or Europe of shipments that enter the country without certification. Reprocessing pepper shipments after arrival reduces bacterial contamination to safe levels. Reprocessed pepper is certified when processing has been completed. Fumigation with gasses, steam treatment, and gamma radiation, are used to sterilize contaminated pepper.

Fumigation takes place in two stages. Ethylene dibromide is used to kill insects (or their eggs) followed by ethylene oxide (EO) or propylene oxide (PO) gas treatment to destroy microbes. The effectiveness of the EO treatments depends on moisture content, temperature, gas concentration, and time. EO can be administered at low pressure after a vacuum has been created, or under high pressure using an inert gas for dilution to the required concentration. The EO and PO gasses are explosive and toxic to humans, and fumigant gas residues may remain in the pepper. Residual gases are minimized by a period of aeration; however, traces of non-gaseous metabolites (molecules that are created when EO reacts with naturally occurring compounds found in pepper), such as ethylene glycol and ethylene chlorohydrin, may remain. Fumigation can be used only on bulk pepper (not packaged), and the organoleptic properties of the pepper may be affected by residues. Fumigation of pepper is approved in the United States (since 2001), and it is popular with spice companies because products that have been fumigated do not have to be labeled as such. Pepper labeled "organic" is not fumigated. Fumigation is banned in many European countries, although they are increasingly under pressure to allow it.

Steam sterilization is a form of pasteurization. In order to be effective, the steam must be applied under pressure multiple times with cooling periods in between. It is most effective on surface contamination. There is product degradation when steam treatment is used; however, no toxic residues are left behind. After steam treatment, the pepper needs to be dried to prevent mold and mycotoxin production. Steam treatment is expensive and is primarily used by countries that do not permit EO fumigation or irradiation. Steam-treated pepper may be labeled "organic" because no chemicals are used in the process.

By far the most effective method to reduce bacterial contaminants is irradiation. Irradiated pepper is bacteria free, with negligible degradation in quality or presence of residuals. Irradiation uses concentrated beams of gamma radiation emitted from a Cobalt-60 source, the same source of radiation used in cancer treatments. It is equally effective on bulk or packaged products, and is very low cost compared to other sterilization methods. Irradiated food products (including pepper) must be labeled as such. In the EU, the product is labeled "ionized." The "Radura" symbol is used on products sold in the United States. More than fifty countries permit irradiation of foods. Foods containing irradiated pepper are not required to use the Radura symbol. Despite the significant advantages of irradiation, some consumers believe it is dangerous (radioactive), and spice companies prefer to use fumigation (even though it is by far the most damaging and dangerous) because it requires no labeling at all. Other methods of bacteria elimination such as dry heat, microwave radiation, high-pressure processing, supercritical CO_2, ozone, and pulsed light are being evaluated.

Pesticide and heavy metal contamination has been shown to be present in peppercorns. However, given the small amounts (by weight) of pepper consumed by individuals, and low levels of contamination, the risk assessment for these contaminants is low. Except for highly concentrated forms of pepper (such as oleoresin or piperine) where the manufacturing process can also concentrate the contaminant, toxicology testing is unnecessary.

It is wrong to assume that at this stage in the proceedings, pepper is completely safe. Every step in supply chain has risks that must be minimized in order to protect consumers. Cross-contamination in grinding machines, spice blending, and packaging lines can reintroduce bacteria to the final product.

Quality

After the product is deemed microbiologically safe and free from filth, the next matter of interest is adulteration of pepper. The American Spice Trade Association (ASTA) defines adulteration as the "inclusion in foods of constituents whose presence is prohibited by regulation, custom, and practice or making impure by adding inferior, alien or less desirable materials or elements. Adulteration can also include the removal of a valuable constituent."[5] The FDA also specifies that a product must be true to how it is represented (if the label says pepper, then it must be pepper and only pepper), and that no volatile oil or component has been removed.

In the case of pepper, adulteration primarily involves adding a less costly constituent for purposes of financial gain. The most common adulterant of pepper is papaya seeds. Dried papaya seeds resemble peppercorns in size, color and wrinkled surface. As much as two parts papaya seed may be mixed with one part peppercorns in Indian street markets. If your peppercorns lack pungency and aroma, you can easily test for the presence of papaya seeds: they float in water; pepper sinks to the bottom. The same test can be done with ground pepper. Put a teaspoon of ground pepper into water. After a few minutes, the pepper will sink to the bottom leaving contaminants or pepper dust floating on top. The water should be clear and transparent. Some disreputable spice sellers will "flour" their spices, adding flour to ground spices to bulk them up. Flour will make the water cloudy. The wary consumer should also know that cheap light berry and pinhead peppercorns are often used to make "pure ground pepper."

There is no standard descriptive grading system for pepper quality. The International Standards Organization (ISO) statement on black pepper (ISO 959-1, 1998[6]) defines black pepper as the dried fruit of the *Piper nigrum* vine with an unbroken pericarp. The corresponding definition for white pepper[7] is the dried fruit of the *Piper nigrum* vine from which the pericarp has been removed. Black pepper products are further classified by the state of processing in the exporting country. For example, "non-processed" means the pepper has not been garbled or cleaned. "Semi-processed" means it has been cleaned, but not graded. "Processed" pepper means the peppercorns have been cleaned and graded and conform to the all definitions of the standard. ISO defines gray pepper as being another name for black pepper. Light berry pepper has reached a normal stage of development but without a kernel (seed) inside. Pinheads are peppercorns of very small size. Broken berry is peppercorns that have been broken into two or more pieces. Extraneous matter is anything that is not pepper. The ISO specifies that ground pepper is made from black pepper and contains no extraneous matter. ISO standard ground pepper will include gray, light berry, broken, pinhead, and older peppercorns because they are cheaper. Ground pepper from reputable spice companies is made from good-quality peppercorns, but seldom from the top quality. If you do not need the convenience of ground pepper, whole peppercorns are your best assurance of obtaining a quality product.

By far, most of the world's pepper is generic. Generic pepper is pungent and in most cases has enough aroma to do the job. The International Pepper Community (IPC) defines pepper as black or white, grade 1 or grade 2. The difference between grade 1 and 2 peppercorns is the density, moisture, and percentage of light or damaged berries. No distinction is made as to the size of the peppercorns. Generic pepper may be a mixture of peppercorns from a single or multiple countries. It is relatively low in cost and available everywhere.

Regional Differences

Special-quality peppercorns are usually named after a region of production. Some have been awarded protected designation of origin (PGO), protected geographic indication (PGI) or traditional specialities guaranteed (TSG) status by the EU. Peppercorns from different regions have different aromas due to the soil, climate, plant variety, and processing methods. Much like the AOC system used to label wines, none of the protected designations guarantee a level of quality (although quality tends to be very good). They

Table 8.1.   International Pepper Community Grades

Quality Parameter	Black Pepper (Whole)		White Pepper (Whole)	
	IPC BP-1	IPC BP-2	IPC WP-1	IPC WP-2
MACRO				
1. Bulk Density (g/l, min.)	550	500	600	600
2. Moisture (% vol/wt, max.)	12	14	13	15
3. Light Berries/Corns (% by wt, max.)	2	10	1	2
4. Extraneous Matter (% by wt, max.)	1	2	1	2
5. Black Berries/Corns (% by wt, max)	n/a	n/a	1	2
6. Moldy Berries/Corns (% by wt, max.)	1	3	1	3
7. Insect-Defiled Berries/ Corns (% by wt, max)	1	2	1	2
8. Whole Insects, Dead or Alive (by count, max)	Not more than 2 numbers in each subsample and not more than 5 numbers in total subsamples.		Not more than 2 numbers in each subsample and not more than 5 numbers in total subsamples.	
9. Mammalian or/and Other Excreta (by count, max)	Shall be free of any visible mammalian or/and other excreta.		Shall be free of any visible mammalian or/and other excreta.	
MICROBIOLOGICAL				
1. Aerobic Plate Count (Colony Forming Unit/g)	5×10^4	5×10^4	5×10^4	5×10^4
2. Mold and Yeast (Colony Forming Unit/g)	1×10^3	1×10^3	1×10^3	1×10^3
3. *Escherichia coli* (Most Probable Number/g)	< 3	< 3	< 3	< 3
4. Salmonella (Detection / 25 g)	Negative	Negative	Negative	Negative

IPC BP-2 and IPC WP-2 are grades of pepper that has been partially processed (i.e., has gone through some basic cleaning processes like sieving and winnowing). IPC BP-1 and IPC WP-1 are grades of pepper that has been further processed (i.e., has gone through further cleaning processes including sieving, cycloning, destining, washing, and mechanical drying).

simply guarantee that the peppercorns come from the designated region and are produced using the traditional methods employed in the region.

White pepper is mainly produced in Indonesia (Sarawak) and Malaysia (Muntok). It is also produced in India and the Cameroon (Penja). Sarawak pepper is grown in Malaysia on the island of Borneo. Both white and black pepper are produced here. Sarawak has defined its own standards.[8] "Naturally Clean Black Pepper" is the name given to top-quality Sarawak pepper that features very low microbial counts. The "Sarawak Extra Bold Black Pepper" grade is similar in size to Tellicherry peppercorns (4.5 mm). The top grade of white pepper, called "Sarawak Creamy White," features large berry sizes (4.0 mm) and a strong pungent taste with pine-like notes in the aroma. Many aficionados feel it is the world's best white pepper.

Muntok white pepper is most common type of white peppercorns in the world. Good-quality peppercorns from Muntok are creamy-white, strongly pungent, with a fermented or slight eucalyptus aroma. Muntok white peppercorns are smaller than Sarawak.

Lampung (also called Lampong) pepper comes from Sumatra. The peppercorns are small, dark in color with a matte luster. They are very pungent, but not aromatic. A great deal of Lampung pepper is certified organic.

Most spice-trade professionals agree the best pepper in the world is Malabar pepper. The Malabar designation has been granted registration under the Geographic Registration of Goods Act of 1999. Malabar is primarily associated with Kerala, but includes all of south India, the traditional lands of the Madras presidency. The Indian system of grading pepper includes pepper grades from other regions of India. It is much more precise

Table 8.2.   Indian Black Pepper Grades

Grade	Size (mm)	Extraneous Matter	Light Berries	Moisture Content	Description
TGSEB	> 4.75	0.5%	3%	11%	Tellicherry Garbled Special Extra Bold
TGEB	> 4.25	0.5%	3%	11%	Tellicherry Garbled Extra Bold
TG	> 4.0	0.5%	3%	11%	Tellicherry Garbled
MG-1	> 3.25	0.5%	2%	11%	Malabar Garbled Grade 1
MG-2	< 3.25	0.5%	5%	11%	Malabar Garbled Grade 2
MUG-1	n/a	2.0%	7%	12%	Malabar Ungarbled Grade 1
MUG-2	n/a	2.0%	10%	12%	Malabar Ungarbled Grade 2
MUG-3L	n/a	3.0%	15%	12%	Malabar Ungarbled Grade 3 Light
MUG-4L	n/a	4.0%	20%	12%	Malabar Ungarbled Grade 4 Light
GLS	n/a	2.0%	0	0%	Garbled Light Special
GL-1	n/a	3.0%	< 5%	5%	Garbled Light 1
GL-2	n/a	5.0%	< 10%	10%	Garbled Light 2
GL-3	n/a	6.0%	< 15%	15%	Garbled Light 3
UGLS	n/a	3.9%	0	12%	Ungarbled Light Special
UG-1	n/a	4.0%	< 5%	12%	Ungarbled Light 1
UG-2L	n/a	7.0%	< 10%	12%	Ungarbled Light 2

Percentages are by weight. Extraneous matter includes pinheads. Fifty percent of light berries will float in 80 percent alcohol solution.

than the grading system used by the IPC, providing standards for sixteen grades of pepper.

The famous Tellicherry peppercorns are simply large Malabar peppercorns. They come from the same vine as smaller peppercorns and are harvested at the same time. As fans of Godzilla know, size really does matter. As peppercorns grow larger, they have less heat (pungency) and more aroma. The reverse is true for smaller peppercorns. Tellicherry peppercorns are famous for the near-perfect balance of aroma and pungency. Because pepper in cooked food loses aroma, Tellicherry peppercorns are ideal for tempering. They are a great choice for the pepper grinder at the table. The top quality of Indian pepper is TGSEB: Tellicherry Garbled Special Extra Bold. Ninety-five percent of these peppercorns are 4.75 mm or larger in diameter. The citrus (lime, lemon, and orange) notes are readily apparent in the aroma. The word "bold" in the description refers to the aroma, not the pungency. The heat is medium, allowing for a generous grind at the table without adding excessive pungency to the dish. Some pepper grinders do not readily accept the large TGSEB peppercorns (up to 5.5 mm in diameter).

The next-best category is TGEB (the word "special" is no longer included in the description). TGEB peppercorns are slightly smaller, with 95 percent of peppercorns 4.25 mm in diameter or larger. All Tellicherry pepper is free from mold and insects, with < 0.5 percent extraneous matter, < 3 percent light berries (by weight), and < 11 percent moisture content and a minimum weight of 530 grams per liter. Indus Organics (California) has named a super-large "Tellicherry Garbled Special Extra Bold Jumbo" grade. Although not an officially recognized grade, these giants among peppercorns are a minimum of 5.5 mm in diameter. Overly zealous buyers attracted to these incredibly large peppercorns need to ensure that their peppermills can handle them.

Many chefs will choose Malabar MG-1 or MG-2 pepper for the kitchen, as it has plenty of pungency, good aroma, and significantly lower cost. The MG-1 grade has 95 percent of the peppercorns a minimum of 3.35 mm in diameter and the maximum weight is 550 grams per liter. MG-2 is similar, with slightly smaller berries. Progressively lower grades include MUG-1 and MUG-2, followed by MUG 3L and MUG-4L. The quality goes lower as the grade numbers go higher due to increased extraneous matter (up to 4 percent), light berries (up to 20 percent) and 12 percent moisture content. Any Malabar pepper below the grade of MG-2 is used in ground pepper, or is processed to produce oleoresin and piperine.

Buying pepper for personal use can be as easy as going to a local store and picking it up, or ordering it on the internet. If you are looking to obtain special quality, named pepper, it can be challenging to find them in stores. On the internet, hundreds of vendors sell named pepper varieties. However, there is very little to guarantee that the pepper you get is what you think you are buying. Dealing with reputable suppliers is the only way to be sure. If you are buying Tellicherry pepper, measuring the size will help confirm that you have the real thing. It is a simple matter to count out ten peppercorns and line them up along a ruler. Real TGSEB pepper will measure 4.7 cm or more. TGEB peppercorns will be more than 4.25 cm. Anything smaller is Malabar MG-1 or even MG-2. However, are the peppercorns really from Malabar? Buyers should be aware that Vietnam also produces large (5.0 mm) peppercorns, sold as "Vietnam Bold."

Of greater concern is the proportion of light berry pepper. Light berry peppercorns are visually indistinguishable from regular black peppercorns. When peppercorns grow and mature, a small number fail to develop the seed inside (with the exception of light berries from Sri Lanka that have been harvested several months early to prevent theft). The only way to check light berry content is to put a sample of peppercorns into 80 percent alcohol. The peppercorns that float are light berries. In the United States, Everclear 151 proof is a branded product that contains 75.5 percent alcohol and is suitable for the test at home. Simply count out one hundred peppercorns and see how may float. If the specification for your pepper is 3 percent light berry or less, then all but three peppercorns should sink to the bottom.

Most of the world's peppercorns are of a similar (small) size. The laws regulating the importation of pepper into many producing countries are lax, enabling traders to import pepper from other producers, and then sell it as their own.[9] Demand for pepper from Sarawak exceeds their production, and importing pepper to be resold as "Sarawak" is more lucrative to cunning entrepreneurs than increasing the acreage of plantations. Despite these cautions, specialty pepper is available from trustworthy suppliers locally or on the internet. You may never know if the pepper you purchased is the real thing or not, but it may not matter. If the pepper is good, and has the characteristics you want, it does not matter where it came from.

Cooking with Pepper **9**

WHOLE PEPPERCORNS ARE USED in certain prepared meats and cold meat dishes like aspics (gelatin), pâtés, or terrines. They are also used in infusions such as spiced oils or vinegars. Most often, pepper is cracked, crushed, or ground before use. By now, readers know that pepper aroma and taste is best when fresh, whole peppercorns are processed just before use. The purpose of this chapter is to provide understanding of the devices used to grind pepper in the kitchen and at the table, followed by some thoughts about cooking with pepper. Pepper is widely used in many recipes, but some recipes feature pepper as a dominant flavor. This was never intended to be a cookbook; however, at the end of the chapter there is a sampling of recipes that highlight pepper. The recipes in this chapter are organized by the type of pepper (green, black, white, and red). Some of the recipes are classics, some illustrate different ways that pepper is used, and a few were chosen because they originate from the same places where pepper grows. The idea is that after trying some of these recipes, the differences in flavor, aroma, and combinations of tastes will be more apparent. Besides, having made it to the end of this book, the real fun is actually cooking with pepper.

Buying and Storing Peppercorns

Whole peppercorns retain their pungency and aroma much better than many flavoring agents found in the kitchen. Some suppliers suggest you can keep them for up to ten years. That may be so. After all, the pharaohs' noses contain peppercorns that have survived for more than two thousand years; however, at this point they have probably lost their pungency and aroma. Fresher pepper is always going to be better than older pepper. The strategy to enjoy your pepper as fresh as possible begins with the source. It has to be fresh when you buy it. Avoid bulk stores and unknown, often discounted brands of prepackaged peppercorns, and definitely throw out the peppercorns that came with your shiny, new pepper grinder. These peppercorns are virtually guaranteed to be of low quality, and may have been resting there for a long time. There is a lot you can check before bringing your purchase home. The label should indicate where the pepper comes from (for example, product of India, product of Vietnam, etc.) and if it is a named variety (like Malabar, Sarawak, or Lampung). If it does not say any of these things, it probably comes from any number of producing countries, and may be a mixture of commodity-traded pepper from many countries. If the label indicates that it has been irradiated (Radura symbol or the words "ionized"), it will be better than pepper that has been sterilized with steam. Steam-processed (organic) pepper has been subjected to heat and moisture, sure-fire ways to lose some pungency and aroma. If nothing on the label indicates how it was sterilized, you may safely assume it has been fumigated. Fumigated pepper is of good quality and is not likely to have enough residue to cause any health problems, especially since the amount of pepper we use is quite small.

Look for a packing date or best-before date on the container. The packaging date is usually printed on the container (not the label) and may be hard to see. Look on the side of the container near the top or bottom. Breathing moist air on the container helps reveal the date. Jars or plastic containers that have a seal under the cap are indicative of better quality inside, as are vacuum-sealed plastic bags. Opaque (foil-laminated plastic or tins) packaging, while not essential, is indicative of extra care taken by the shipper.

Check the size of the peppercorns (Tellicherry peppercorns should be 4.5 mm or larger), the number of white heads visible, and the amount of dust and broken peppercorns in the bottom. Premium-quality peppercorns will have been well garbled, with few (if any) white heads, dust particles, or broken berries in the jar. There should be nothing else visible in the container.

When you get your purchase home, you can test for light berries by putting a sample of one hundred peppercorns in 80 percent alcohol (Everclear) and see how many float (should be less than 3 percent). The floaters are light berries or, in very rare cases, papaya seeds. Clean your pepper grinder of any residual pepper thoroughly and then grind some of the new peppercorns into your hand. The aroma should be readily apparent; it should taste strongly pungent immediately, then fade out slowly on your tongue. Once you have found a reliable source of the peppercorns you like, it is better to buy smaller amounts more frequently than to buy a large amount every other year. Most users of pepper in the home will use less than eight ounces (226 grams) of peppercorns per year. Buying fifty grams four or five times a year will cost you more money, but you will enjoy better pepper than buying a pound (454 grams) every second year.

Don't buy a peppermill that holds a large amount of pepper, and remember to clean it out between fillings. Partially ground pepper in the bottom of the mill attracts moisture and will cake up. Peppermills are poor storage containers. It is better to refill your peppermill often from a container that is air tight and stored in a cool, dry, dark place. All chemical reactions take place more slowly in cool environments. The aroma of pepper comes from its essential oils. These are volatile and released into the atmosphere over time. A tightly sealed jar retains the aroma and prevents the oils from becoming rancid through exposure to oxygen. Pepper loses its pungency as chavicine converts to piperine. This conversion speeds up when the pepper is exposed to light. Even fluorescent light can photo-isomerize the chavicine and reduce pungency. If you choose to buy in bulk, put your stash in a freezer bag, suck out the air with a straw, and keep it in the freezer. If you buy ground pepper, the same ideas apply. By now, you should have stopped buying ground pepper: it just isn't worth it.

Preparing Peppercorns in the Kitchen

In general, the amounts of pepper needed in various grinds are much smaller at the dining room table than in the kitchen. Pepper grinders that belong in the dining room are pressed into kitchen service; however, there are other, more efficient methods of reducing a teaspoon or more of whole peppercorns to the right-size granules. Besides being slow, dining table grinders do not do a good job on cracked or very course grinds of pepper that are almost exclusively used in the kitchen.

The mortar and pestle is one of the oldest kitchen tools in the world. Archeologists have found examples that are thirty-five thousand years old. They were used by the early peoples on every continent, in much the same way as they are today. In addition to pounding and grinding food, it was used to prepare medicines. The immortalized mortar and pestle symbol appears on many modern pharmacies, a reminder of the days when apothecaries ground and blended ingredients into medicines on a custom basis. The mortar is a weighty, bowl-shaped utensil with a sturdy base made from wood, stone, or ceramic materials. The pestle is like a small club or baseball bat, usually made from the same material as the mortar. It is used to smash into submission almost any kind of food, wet or dry, hard or soft, herb or spice, turning it into a paste, powder, or any texture in between. Some mortars are smooth inside, others have a rough surface that helps hold the ingredients in place while they are bashed and ground to perfection. By crushing, smashing, and grinding, flavors trapped inside the ingredients are released and blended to deliver the freshest, most aromatic flavor to the next step in the proceedings.

Cracking whole peppercorns takes place by using the pestle to exert pressure on peppercorns placed inside the mortar. Sounds simple, but there are a few things to keep in mind. To crack pepper, it is simply a matter of pressing the pestle onto a few peppercorns with just enough force to break the berries into two or three pieces.[1] Pounding will pulverize parts of the peppercorns, yielding a quantity of pepper dust. Processing a small number of peppercorns at a time ensures that the peppercorns are uniformly cracked. Recipes that call for cracked pepper do so because the pepper flavor and aroma release slowly as the food is cooked, or rests. Using pepper that is broken into very small particles leads to a quick release of aroma that may not have enough time to be absorbed by the food being prepared. Continuing to work the pestle using a grinding action with crushing pressure reduces the peppercorns to a progressively finer powder. The combination of crushing and grinding action releases volatile essential oils and fills the kitchen area with a warm, musty tantalizing aroma. Ground pepper is not the only way the mortar and pestle is used. After reducing the size of the pepper particles to the desired consistency, a small amount of butter added to the mortar turns it into a paste that captures the aroma and taste released when added to warm food. By grinding a mixture of spices including pepper together in the mortar, it is possible to produce a seasoning mix with well-integrated flavors. Depending on its size, a mortar and pestle is used to prepare a substantial amount (fifty grams or more) of pepper at a time: handy if you are making large batches. While it is an excellent tool in the kitchen, it is too large and awkward for use at the dining table.

Modern times being what they are, small electric grinders are available in sizes suitable for grinding a couple of tablespoons of peppercorns at a time. These grinders use a high-speed rotating blade with a flat edge. They work like a hammer mill by repeatedly hitting the pepper with the flat edge of the blade, breaking it into progressively smaller pieces. The instructions recommend pulsing the grinder to get the best effect. They are very fast, and it takes practice to get the size of grind you want. Ground pepper made with an electric mill is often inconsistent due to the substantive amount of pepper dust produced. The best way to get a consistent grind is by passing the pepper through a sieve to get rid of the dust. Electric grinders are useful for grinding larger amounts of pepper if you are making a stew or batch of sausages. They are also handy for combining a number of spices to be crushed and blended at the same time. Unlike the mortar and pestle, small electric spice grinders are noisy. Small food-processing machines (for example, those made by Cuisinart) can be used to grind spices; however, even the smallest ones tend to work badly unless they are filled with a substantial quantity of peppercorns. They have the same shortcomings as the hand-held versions: inconsistent particle size. Crank-operated coffee grinders can be used to grind pepper if you need large quantities. They do a good job of delivering consistent batches of coarse-, medium-, or fine-ground pepper.

Grinding Pepper at the Table

Pepper is used at the dining table as a condiment; consequently, much smaller amounts of pepper are needed on an individual basis. Handheld peppermills are a much better alternative than pepper shakers filled with ground pepper. There are several technologies suitable for handheld pepper grinder designs. The most common pepper grinders use burr mill technology. A burr mill involves two counter-rotating cone-shaped surfaces (one male, the other female) with burrs (cutting edges) that cut shavings from the item being ground. The closer the two surfaces get, the finer the shavings. Burr mills operate in only one direction (clockwise). Burr mill technologies generate much less heat than technologies that use abrasive or friction methods to reduce the size of the peppercorn. If the burrs are sharp, very little force is needed to operate the mill and pepper particles are uniform in size. Most pepper mills using burr mill technology are operated by a drive shaft that connects the rotating top with the grinding mechanism located below the pepper reservoir. Some designs use a crank instead of the rounded top; others are driven by an electric motor and feature a small light in the base to allow you to see how much pepper is being dispensed when used in darkened rooms.

Most burr mill pepper grinders are based on a design patented by Peugeot in 1842. The Peugeot design is a two-stage burr mill, where large grooves between the burrs at the top of the mill hold and crush the peppercorns, followed by smaller grooves that progressively grind the pepper to its final size. Many consider the Peugeot peppermill to be the best in the world. It lasts forever (Peugeot's grinding mechanism is guaranteed for life), and the adjustable grind from coarse to fine yields very consistently sized pepper particles. The ample grooves will accommodate large TGSEB-size peppercorns (up to 5 mm in diameter).

Burr mill peppermills are manufactured from a number of different materials. The Peugeot mills use case-hardened steel. The sharp burrs and deep grooves are cut when the steel is soft and then hardened to retain sharpness for a long time. Although the case-hardening treatment also inhibits corrosion, carbon steel mills should not be used in a steamy environment such as above a boiling pot. Corrosion will dull the burrs long before the mill shows signs of trouble. Using the mill over steaming pots and pans can clog your mill because moisture easily cakes up finely ground pepper. If you like to use your peppermill over a steaming pot or frying pan, stainless or ceramic construction is a good choice. Stainless-steel burr mills are more corrosion resistant; however, they do not retain the sharp-

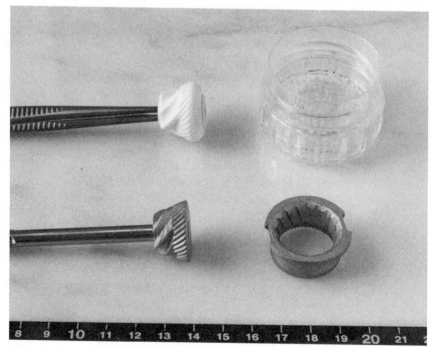

Photo 9.1.   Case-hardened steel, ceramic, and acrylic burr grinder mechanisms. Simon Day

ness of the burrs quite as well as those with carbon steel construction. Chrome-plated zinc alloy is used to make lower-cost peppermills. Zinc alloy mills work fine when new, but do not last nearly as long as carbon or stainless-steel mechanisms. Metal burr mills should never be used with highly corrosive salt. Corrosion-proof burr mills are made of ceramic or acrylic material. Ceramic mechanisms are extremely hard and last a long time unless a foreign substance (like a grain of sand or a small stone) enters the mill, destroying the cutting edges. The edges of the ceramic mills are not as sharp as case-hardened steel; however, ceramic mills work well. Unlike metal mills, ceramic mills can be used to grind salt.

Acrylic burr mills have become popular with spice companies that sell pepper in packaging with a disposable grinder top. Acrylic is a thermoset plastic (hardens when heated). It is not as durable as metal or ceramic, and some spice bottles are designed with the outer burr ring molded right in, making it impossible to refill them. When the spice is used up, you buy a new bottle, complete with the grinding mechanism. Acrylic burr mills are very low cost to produce and do not have to grind more than a few ounces of pepper before being thrown away or recycled. One manufacturer of spice bottles says that the cost difference between a regular spice bottle with a flip-top closure and one fitted with an acrylic grinding mechanism is negligible.[2] Advanced designs of disposable pepper grinders include the ability to adjust the grind. The grind quality of disposable mill caps is inferior to metal or ceramic mills.

Another approach to grinding pepper is using friction and abrasion. Several designs (Rabbit, Chef'n Pepperball, etc.) use this principle with a two-levered hand-actuated mechanism. Unlike the regular pepper grinder designs, the two-levered actuator system makes it possible to grind pepper using only one hand. A platen with small dimples holds a few peppercorns and rubs them against a stainless-steel rasp. The ground pepper drops out the bottom. Some of these mills are adjustable and do a reasonably good job grinding coarse pepper. The system uses friction to hold the peppercorns in place and generates more heat than a burr-grinding method. Therein lies the joy in using this kind of grinder. A substantive amount of tantalizing aroma is released into the air as the grinder does its work. On the negative side, it takes a lot of squeezing cycles to get a small amount of pepper. These are not a good tool for individuals who like a lot of pepper, although it is probably good exercise for people who want to exercise their grip while seated at the dinner table. Some users report that the actuating mechanism is not sufficiently robust and prone to breakage.

Cooking Methods and Pepper

Piperine is the component of pepper that provides the sharp, pungent taste. When cooking with pepper, it is important to remember that piperine is highly soluble in fats and alcohol, and to a lesser degree in acids such as vinegar or lemon juice. Water absorbs very little piperine. Fats and alcohol capture aromas; however, these are released when heat is applied. Foods cooked or stewed for a time will lose the pepper aroma but not the pungency. Restoring the pepper aroma is as simple as grinding some fresh pepper onto the food just before serving or at the table.

When food is cooked with pepper, the fineness of the grind plays a role in how the flavor and aroma develops. For roasting or stewing, a slow release of the aroma and taste is best using cracked peppercorns. As it cooks, the piperine and aromatic components are released slowly into surrounding fats. Cracked pepper should be applied to the top of the roast. As the fat melts and drips down the sides of a roast, it absorbs the aroma and pungency from the peppercorns and transfers it to the meat over time. In the case of a stew, fats in the cooking liquid absorb piperine from the cracked peppercorns gradually and infuse the food with aroma and taste. To avoid having cracked peppercorns in the food at time of service, they are put into a little cheesecloth or muslin bag like a bouquet garni. Finely ground pepper releases its aroma and pungency quickly. Best used after cooking is complete, the release of aroma is instantaneous. Given that the aroma is lost quickly during cooking, some chefs will use white peppercorns for cooking, and finish with finely ground black pepper for the aroma.

Recipes for Green Peppercorns

Use canned green peppercorns in brine for these recipes. Rinse before using.

Green Peppercorn Cream Sauce

Ingredients:

- 1 teaspoon olive oil
- 1 Tablespoon finely chopped shallot
- 2 Tablespoons green peppercorns
- 2 × 1 Tablespoons unsalted butter
- 2 Tablespoons brandy
- 1 Tablespoon Worcestershire Sauce (substitute: soy sauce)
- ½ cup low-salt beef broth
- ½ cup heavy (whipping) cream
- 2 teaspoons flour
- Salt

Instructions:

1. Heat the oil in a saucepan over medium-high heat until it shimmers. Add the chopped shallot, peppercorns, and 1 Tablespoon of the butter and cook briefly (30 seconds).
2. Add the brandy without setting it alight. Reduce heat. Use a wooden scraping tool to scrape any browned bits from the bottom of the saucepan. Stir in the Worcestershire sauce.
3. Add the broth, stir to combine, and bring to a slow boil. Cook for 5 minutes.
4. Add the cream, return to a slow boil, and cook for further 5 minutes, until the mixture becomes slightly creamy.
5. Prepare a *beurre manié* by kneading the flour with the remaining butter. Add to the pan and cook at a slow boil, stirring constantly until thickened.
6. Season with salt to taste. Serve warm.

Comments: Use on filet mignon or boneless rib eye steak; try it on pasta with sautéed mushrooms.

Salmon with Green Peppercorns

Ingredients:

- 2 Tablespoons oil for frying
- 4 × 6 oz boneless center-cut salmon filets
- 2 teaspoons green peppercorns, rinsed and cracked to coarse granules
- 2 Tablespoons lemon juice
- 2 ounces unsalted butter
- Salt

Instructions:

1. Heat oil in non-stick frying pan over medium-high heat until it shimmers
2. Sear salmon on both sides (1½ minutes per side); reduce heat and cook until center is barely translucent.
3. Remove the pan from heat and transfer salmon to individual warmed plates.
4. Put lemon juice, butter, and crushed peppercorns in the pan and stir to incorporate.
5. Lightly sprinkle salmon filets with salt and top with 2 teaspoons of pan sauce

Comment: Try this recipe with black peppercorns and compare.

Shrimp with Green Peppercorns

Ingredients:

- 5 or 6 bamboo skewers, soaked in water
- 1 lb raw, peeled jumbo shrimp (21–25 per pound)
- 2 Tablespoons green peppercorns (rinsed)
- 5–7 curry leaves (fresh if possible). Do not substitute curry powder. It is not the same thing.
- 2 teaspoons grated ginger
- 1 medium clove of garlic crushed
- ½ teaspoon salt
- ¼ teaspoon ground turmeric
- 2 teaspoons lime juice (about 1 lime)
- 2 Tablespoons oil

Instructions:

1. Crush and amalgamate green peppercorns, curry leaves, ginger, garlic, turmeric, lime juice, and salt with a mortar and pestle.
2. Marinate shrimp in the mixture for 1 hour.
3. Thread 4 shrimp on each skewer, leaving enough room for a handle at the dull end.
4. Amalgamate the oil with any remaining marinade.
5. Cook on a hot BBQ (or grill pan) for 1 minute per side (until the center is just past the translucent stage). Brush with oil/marinade mixture. Do not overcook!

Comments: South Asian grocery stores (India, Sri Lanka) are your best source for curry leaves. Substitute dried curry leaves (internet suppliers) if fresh ones are unavailable.

Recipes for Black Peppercorns

Singapore-Style Black Pepper Crab

Ingredients:

- 2 oz (½ stick) unsalted butter
- 3 cloves garlic, chopped into ⅛-inch cubic pieces
- 3 green onions, chopped into ¼-inch pieces
- 2 Tablespoon black pepper, cracked into medium-sized granules
- 3 pounds thawed, previously frozen cooked crab legs (king or snow) or claws (Jonah or stone); cut legs into 3-inch pieces. Thaw immediately before use.
- 1 Tablespoon oyster sauce
- 2 Tablespoons water
- 1 Tablespoon sugar

Instructions:

1. Sauté garlic and green onion in butter for 1 minute (in a wok), then add cracked black pepper.
2. Add crab and toss to coat evenly with pepper mixture. Heat through.
3. Add oyster sauce, water, and sugar, and stir continuously to coat the crab evenly.
4. Turn off heat and cover with a lid for 3 minutes to allow the crab to absorb flavors.
5. Toss again and serve immediately.

Comments: Crab is eaten with the fingers and is messy, so you need plenty of paper napkins. Traditional recipes use live mud crabs farmed in India. Live Dungeness crab, killed, cleaned, and cut into quarters also works well.

COOKING WITH PEPPER   143

Indonesian Style Black Pepper Beef

Ingredients:

- 1 pound flank steak, thinly sliced across the grain
- 3 Tablespoons soy sauce
- 1 Tablespoon Chinese rice wine
- 1 teaspoon sesame oil
- 1 Tablespoon black pepper, finely ground.
- 2 Tablespoons oil
- 3 cloves garlic, minced
- 1 Tablespoon finely sliced ginger
- 1 onion, cut into wedges
- 1 red bell pepper, seeded and thinly sliced
- ½ teaspoon salt
- 1 Tablespoon brown sugar
- 1 Tablespoon oyster sauce
- 1 Tablespoon corn starch + 3 Tablespoons water, mixed well
- 3 green onions, cut into ½-inch pieces

Instructions:

1. Marinate the beef in soy sauce, rice wine, sesame oil, and black pepper for 2 hours.
2. Sauté garlic and ginger in a wok for 2 minutes with oil, then add onion and cook until translucent.
3. Add beef to the wok, and stir fry until cooked through.
4. Add red bell pepper, salt, brown sugar, and oyster sauce.
5. Thicken with cornstarch and water mixture, toss well, remove from heat.
6. Serve with plain white rice and garnish with green onions on top.

Comment: This Indonesian-inspired dish is a natural for hotter-tasting Sarawak black pepper.

Hakka–Style Pepper Chicken Thighs

Ingredients:

- 2 pounds chicken thighs with skin and bone-in (substitute: drumsticks)
- 1 Tablespoon ground black pepper
- 2 Tablespoons dark, full-salt soy sauce
- Cilantro, coarsely chopped

Instructions:

1. Pierce with chicken with a fork in several places. Coat the chicken with a mixture of soy sauce and ground black pepper. Rub the chicken, working the mixture under the skin as much as possible.
2. Use a large frying pan, skillet, or Dutch oven with a lid. Place the chicken into the pan in a single layer, covering the bottom of the pan.
3. Pour in remaining soy sauce/pepper mixture.
4. Cook covered on medium-low heat for 15 minutes, then turn chicken over. There should be liquid in the pan. Add a few ounces of water if needed.
5. Continue cooking covered under low heat for 15–20 minutes until done.
6. Remove chicken to a platter, scrape and reduce pan juices then pour on top.
7. Garnish with plenty of cilantro on top.

Comments: The Hakka are Chinese Han people who migrated south to India many centuries ago. There are still vibrant Hakka Chinese communities in India. Hakka cuisine is a fusion of Indian and Chinese cooking that has recently grown in popularity.

Strawberries with Cracked Pepper

Ingredients:

- 1 pound fresh, ripe strawberries (local, in season if possible)
- 1 teaspoon sugar
- ½ teaspoon coarse cracked black pepper
- 2 oz Grand Marnier liqueur (substitute Triple Sec)
- ¼ teaspoon vanilla extract, or inside scrapings of 2 vanilla beans
- Whipped cream (spray bomb or homemade)

Instructions:

1. Wash, then cut strawberries in half or quarters
2. Using a mortar and pestle, crack the peppercorns into large granules.
3. Put strawberries, crackled pepper, sugar, liqueur, and vanilla extract into a bowl. Toss to coat well. If using vanilla beans, slice the beans in half lengthwise and scrape the inside of the beans. Put the scrapings into the bowl.
4. Put into the refrigerator and marinate for 30 minutes, tossing occasionally.
5. Serve with whipped cream.

Comments: This recipe depends on very coarsely cracked pepper particles. Use the largest, freshest Tellicherry peppercorns you can find for best results.

Black Pepper–Infused Vodka

Ingredients:

- Tablespoon cracked peppercorns
- 750 ml vodka (40 percent alcohol)

Other ingredients for cocktails:

- Ice
- Beef bouillon
- Tomato juice
- Lemon juice
- Lemon peel
- Worcestershire sauce

Instructions:

1. Using a mortar and pestle, crack peppercorns once into 2 or 3 pieces.
2. Put the peppercorns inside the vodka bottle and reseal.
3. Store at room temperature for 1 week.

Comments: Piperine will not dissolve in water but readily dissolves in alcohol. The pepper-infused vodka can be substituted for regular vodka in many drinks:

- Pepper Vodkatini: Chill with ice, strain into martini glass, and garnish with lemon peel.
- Pepper Bull shot: Mix 5 ounces of de-fatted, salty beef consommé with 1½ ounces of pepper vodka, dash of lemon juice, dash of Worcestershire Sauce in a tall glass with ice.
- Pepper Vodka Bloody Mary: Mix 5 ounces of tomato juice, dash of Worcestershire sauce, and 1½ ounces of pepper vodka in a tall glass with ice and lemon peel garnish.

Recipe for White Peppercorns

Thandai Spiced Milk

Ingredients:

- 4 cups of 3.25% full-fat milk
- ½ cup of 10% coffee cream
- ¼ cup sugar
- Saffron (a few strands) or substitute ¼ teaspoon turmeric
- 20 white peppercorns
- 10 almonds
- 10 cashews
- 10 pistachios
- 2 Tablespoons poppy seeds
- 2 Tablespoons fennel seeds
- 8 green cardamom pods
- ½ teaspoon rose water (if available)

Instructions:

1. Combine milk, coffee cream, and sugar with saffron, bring to a boil and cool.
2. Using a mortar and pestle (or electric spice grinder), grind the peppercorns, almonds, cashews, pistachios, poppy, fennel, and cardamom pods into a fine powder.
3. Whisk the powdered ingredients together with the cooled milk and put into the refrigerator for 2 hours.
4. Stir in rosewater and pass through a fine strainer into 4 glasses. Garnish with shreds of almonds and rose petals if available. Served very cold without ice.

Comments: Thandai is a traditional drink served during Holi, the Hindu festival of color celebrated primarily in India and Nepal. Rangwali Holi is when people engage in a free-for-all, spraying each other with water and colored powders. Holi occurs in March, the exact date being determined using the Hindu calendar. Crushed marijuana (*bhang*) is often added to the ingredients.

Recipe for Red Peppercorns

Grilled Scallops with Red Peppercorns

Ingredients:

- 8 large, white scallops
- ½ oz oil
- 2 oz butter
- 2 garlic cloves, peeled and thinly sliced
- 2 teaspoons red peppercorns
- Generous pinch of salt
- 2 sprigs of fresh thyme
- 3 Tablespoons 35% cream

Instructions:

1. Preheat a frying pan until hot.
2. Add oil and sear the scallops for 90 seconds on each side.
3. Add butter, garlic, crushed red peppercorns and thyme; cook for 90 seconds, tossing to incorporate.
4. Add cream, stir to incorporate, and cook for a further 90 seconds. Do not overcook.
5. Serve immediately.

Comment: Red peppercorns have a well-developed pungent core, with a slightly sweet pericarp that marries well with the sweetness of the scallops.

Notes

Chapter 1

1. Differences in the color of bell peppers depend on the time of harvest and degree of ripening. Green bell peppers usually (but not always) turn yellow-orange and then red. The *Permagreen* variety maintains its green color even when fully ripe. Red, orange, and yellow bell peppers are often more expensive than the green ones because they take longer to ripen before harvesting.

2. The United States Food and Drug Administration banned the importation of Sichuan peppercorns from 1968 through 2005 because they were found to be capable of carrying the citrus canker virus bacteria, a disease that is difficult to control. American and Brazilian authorities have ordered infected citrus groves destroyed and burned in order to eradicate the canker. The danger is eliminated by heat-treating the seeds.

3. Saffron cultivation was introduced into England in around 1350 CE, and was centered in the southeast. The importance of this crop in the sixteenth and seventeenth centuries is reflected in the name of the town of Saffron Walden.

Chapter 2

1. A pound of pepper consists of approximately nine thousand one hundred peppercorns.

2. During medieval times, pepper was worth as much as an equivalent weight of gold. A single peppercorn, approximately .05 grams, would be worth about $2 today. Even people of modest means during the Middle Ages were able to purchase a single peppercorn to flavor their food from time to time.

3. One hundred grams of black pepper (approximately 2,000 generic peppercorns) has 252 calories, 205 from carbohydrates, 27 from fat, and 19 from protein. See https://www.aqua-calc.com/page/density-table/substance/spices-coma-and-blank-pepper-coma-and-blank-black (accessed March 24, 2018).

4. Hippocrates (460–370 BCE), Plato (348–348 BCE), and Theophrastus (370–285 BCE) all mention the therapeutic uses of pepper in their writings. Later on, Pliny the Elder (23–79 CE) and Dioscordites (40–90 CE) also wrote about the uses of pepper in their books.

5. The mummified body of Rameses II (1301–1213 BCE) was found to contain peppercorns in the nasal cavity.

6. Ruins of the Sabaean waterworks still exist. Twice as long as the Hoover Dam, ruins of the Great Dam of Marib are visible on satellite photos via Google Earth. The Tawila cisterns (open-air water tanks) are located near the modern city of Aden. There were thousands of kilometers of qanats throughout western Asia, some of which are still used today.

7. Saba was one of the longest-surviving ancient kingdoms, being disestablished in 275 CE by the Himyarites after a protracted civil war.

8. Dhows are sailing vessels thought to have come into use on the Arabian Sea as early as 600 BCE. Ancient Arab sailors procured dhows from southern India, which was rich in timber, coir rope, and skilled tradesmen, as well as a source of pepper. Dhows were an important marine development because they were propelled with wind power instead of human rowers. Dhows powered only by sail continue to transport cargoes across the Arabian sea to this day.

9. Early Chinese ships were canoes, rafts, and oared vessels. The junk (a sailing vessel) was developed approximately 300 BCE.

10. The remnants of Darius's canal were discovered by Napoleon Bonaparte in his 1799 Egyptian campaign. Other remnants of ancient canals connecting the Red Sea with the Nile were found by surveyors of the current Suez Canal.

11. Historically, the Levant was defined as the Mediterranean lands east of Italy. The name "Levant" derives from the idea that it is where the sun rises in the east. More recently, Levant refers to the area encompassing Cyprus, Jordan, Lebanon, Syria, Palestine, and the northern Sinai.

12. While pepper was one of the most important items, elephants, tigers, and other livestock destined for public slaughter by gladiators were also transported by ships from India and the east coast of Africa. Many Arab cities were bankrupted by the Roman domination of the spice trade.

13. Pliny the Elder, *The Natural History*, trans. John Bostock and H. T. Riley (London: Taylor and Francis, 1855), accessed March 24, 2018, http://www.perseus.tufts.edu/hopper/text?doc=Perseus%3Atext%3A1999.02.0137%3Abook%3D12%3Achapter%3D14 .

14. Archeologists found pepper, figs, and olives on this site, no doubt to make this dangerous and isolated outpost feel more like home. See: Jona Lendering, "Oberaden," Livius, accessed March 24, 2018, http://www.livius.org/articles/place/oberaden/.

15. Vindolanda is a Roman fort located near Hadrian's Wall, which was built later. The famous Vindolanda tablets are records of transactions made at the fort and specifically refer to "*piper*," the Latin root of *pepper*.

16. Details of the excavation and reconstruction of a horrea piperatum in Ostia, dated 145–150 CE may be viewed at Ostia Topographical Dictionary, accessed March 24, 2018, http://www.ostia-antica.org/regio1/8/8-3.htm.

17. *De materia medica*, a guide to the medical uses of plants by Dioscorides, used extensively for fifteen hundred years after his death, is still consulted today by herbalists.

18. The term "peppercorn rent" persists in law to this day. A peppercorn rent is metaphor for a very small payment, a nominal consideration used to satisfy the requirements for the creation of a legal contract.

19. The journals of Marco Polo, the famous traveler/explorer from Venice in 1298 CE erased a great deal of the misinformation about pepper and the lands where they grew, motivating renewed interest in finding alternate routes in the fourteenth and fifteenth centuries.

20. The spice-trading hub of the world is located in Jew Town, an ancient part of the city of Cochin (Kochi) in India. It is the site of the oldest synagogue in India, built in 1568 on the site of an earlier synagogue built in 1344. Radhanite Jews were the precursor to modern international banking and were essential to international trade.

21. Both Muslims and Jews practice male circumcision, making it easy to identify Christian males who strayed across borders.

22. Joint family entrepreneurism is a culture where the family pools their resources and involvement in business ventures and investments.

23. A Chinese wreck dated 1272 CE (the Song Dynasty) is 114 feet long and 31 feet wide, with a displacement of 375 tons. The fabled Nanjing treasure fleet (1402) included ships over 400 feet long and 150 feet wide, probably the largest wooden vessels ever built.

24. Backwater boat tours on rice boats are a popular tourism activity along the Malabar coast, now the Indian state of Kerala.

Chapter 3

1. The average meat consumption was one hundred kilograms per person per year: the equivalent of a ten-ounce steak every day. By comparison, this declined to twenty kilograms per person per year in the nineteenth century.

2. Top-quality Tellicherry peppercorns can cost $90 per pound or more from internet specialty suppliers.

3. Prof. John Munro (University of Toronto) provided a comparison of late medieval and current prices paid for spices in terms of an average worker's labor as part of a series of lectures. The comparison can be viewed online at https://www.economics.utoronto.ca/munro5/301LectSummaries.htm. Select PowerPoint slides, Lecture 14, Week 11: 20, November 2013, slide #59 (accessed on March 24, 2018).

4. The Bible refers to the three kings from the orient who came to pay homage to the Christ Child bearing gifts of gold, frankincense, and myrrh, evidence

of early travelers bringing goods with them for gifts and trade. The most famous European traveler was Marco Polo (1254–1324).

5. King Afonso V of Portugal granted a monopoly of trade in the Gulf of Guinea to Lisbon merchant Fernão Gomes in 1469.

6. Amerindian slaves did not turn out to be the source of wealth anticipated due to their lack of resistance to diseases carried by the Spanish conquerors. Most of the Amerindian peoples were efficiently killed off by the introduction of diseases to which they had no resistance.

7. During Columbus's time, estimates of longitude were based on the difference between magnetic north from compass bearings and true north from observations of the North Star. John Harrison invented the chronometer, an extremely accurate clock despite the rocking motion of a ship at sea in 1736. It revolutionized navigation by making it possible to determine a ship's position anywhere in the world, but also to make accurate maps. See David Sobel, *Longitude: The True Story of a Lone Genius Who Solved the Greatest Scientific Problem of His Time* (New York: Bloomsbury, 2005).

8. Some historians argue that the Spanish kings sent Chanca to accompany Columbus to verify and document his findings, there being considerable doubt about his claims regarding the first voyage.

9. The first known settlement, approximately 1000 CE, located at L'Anse aux Meadows in Newfoundland is attributed to the Vikings.

10. Cabral's route took him west to Brazil in order to find favorable winds and avoid the doldrums (Intertropical Convergence Zone), a large mid-Atlantic area that can be without wind for weeks, exhausting the ships' supplies of food and water.

11. A viceroy is a regal appointee with the full power of the king. It literally means "in place of the king."

12. A charter giving similar powers to the Hudson's Bay Company in 1670 allowed it to trade in the drainage basin of Hudson's Bay. The Hudson's Bay Company still exists today as a popular department store in Canada.

13. Larry Collins and Dominique Lapierre, *Freedom at Midnight* (New York: Simon & Schuster, 1976).

14. The Dutch joined forces with the Kingdom of Kandy to remove the Portuguese from Sri Lanka in 1634.

15. An online simulation illustrates the challenges of making a profit trading spices. See http://www.learner.org/interactives/renaissance/spicetrade/arm1.html.

16. Dutch forces invaded Portuguese settlements in Brazil: Bahia (1624) and Pernambuco (1630).

17. In September 1687, 665 slaves were exported by the English from Fort St. George, where Yale was president.

18. As late as the early 1900s, pepper was referred to as "Salem pepper." See New England Historical Society, "Jonathan Carnes Corners the Pepper Market

in 1795," http://www.newenglandhistoricalsociety.com/jonathan-carnes-corners
-pepper-market-1795/.

19. The *Eliza* landed a million pounds (500 tons) of pepper in 1806, only one
of the many ships engaged in the Salem pepper trade. Salem ceased to be a major
center of the pepper trade in 1846 due to an oversupply of pepper the world.

20. See also George Putnam, *A History of the Pepper Trade with the Island of Sumatra* (Salem, MA: Essex Institute, 1922).

21. The Dutch Antilles consist of the Caribbean islands of Aruba, Bonaire,
Curacao, Saint Maarten, Saba, and Sint Eustatius.

Chapter 4

1. Alfons van Gulik, *Pepper Crop Report 2017*, ESA Conference Presentation,
Bordeaux, France, June 1, 2017, accessed March 24, 2018, http://www.nedspice
.com/upload/docs/170601_Nedspice_-_ESA_Pepper_Crop_Report_vFinal.pdf.

2. Surichi Kapur Gomes, "Vietnam Takes the Spice out of India's Curbs on
Pepper: Lankan Pepper Takes Vietnam Route to India, Vietnam Exports Coffee to India via Colombo," *Asian Age*, September 22, 2017, accessed March 24,
2018, http://www.asianage.com/business/in-other-news/220917/vietnam-takes
-the-spice-out-of-indias-curbs-on-pepper.html.

3. "Global Black Pepper Market Will Reach USD 5701.0 Million by 2024,"
Persistence Market Research News Release, Globe Newswire, New York,
September 27, 2017, accessed March 24, 2017, https://globenewswire.com/
news-release/2017/09/27/1133618/0/en/Global-Black-Pepper-Market-will
-Reach-USD-5701-0-Million-by-2024-Persistence-Market-Research.html.

4. Sean Moon, "Herbs, Spices and Seasonings Pack a Powerful Culinary
Punch, Resto Biz, June 28, 2016, accessed March 24, 2018, https://www.restobiz
.ca/herbs-spices-seasonings-pack-powerful-culinary-punch/.

5. Nicole Maunsell, "Canadians Will Spend More in Restaurants in 2018:
Canada's Food Price Report," *Dal News*, Dalhousie University, December 13,
2017, accessed March 24, 2018, https://www.dal.ca/news/2017/12/13/canadians
-will-spend-more-in-restaurants-in-2018—canada-s-food-.html.

6. *Canada's Food Price Report*, Dalhousie University and University of Guelph,
November 27, 2017, accessed March 24, 2018, https://blogs.dal.ca/cfame/
files/2017/12/Canada_Food_Price_Report_Eng_2018_.pdf.

7. Datamonitor, "Changing Cooking Behaviours and Attitudes: Beyond Convenience," cited in *Convenience: Consumer Trend Market Analysis Report 2010*,
Agriculture and Agrifood Canada Online, accessed March 24, 2018, https://
www.gov.mb.ca/agriculture/market-prices-and-statistics/trade-statistics/pubs/
canada_convenience_trend_report_en.pdf.

8. This is by no means a new trend: the 1960s introduced cake mixes and so-
called TV dinners.

9. Maija Kappler, "Meal Kits Grow into $120 Million Industry," *Globe and Mail* (Toronto), December 13, 2017, Accessed March 24, 2018, https://www .theglobeandmail.com/report-on-business/meal-kits-grow-into-120-million -industry-in-canada/article37312803/.

10. Van Gulik, *Pepper Crop Report 2017.*

11. The money multiplier is the price (per ton) divided by the marginal cost of production.

12. S. N. Goswami and O. Challa, "Economic Analysis of Smallholder Rubber Plantations in West Garo Hills District of Meghalaya," *Indian Journal of Agricultural Economics* 62, no. 4 (October–December 2007): 649–63, accessed March 24, 2018, https://ageconsearch.umn.edu/bitstream/204551/2/06-Goswami.pdf.

13. "Struggling Sarawak Pepper Farmers Need Help Due to Falling Prices," *Free Malaysia Today,* July 8, 2017, accessed March 24, 2018, http://www .freemalaysiatoday.com/category/nation/2017/07/08/struggling-sarawak-pepper -farmers-need-help-due-to-falling-prices/.

14. Ajayan, "Indian Pepper Futures' Prices Drop Even as Global Prices Rise," Livemint, April 29, 2007, accessed March 24, 2018, http://www.livemint.com/ Money/gnJkCCxpdd8RozcK825gDI/Indian-pepper-futures-prices-drop-even -as-global-prices-ris.html.

15. "Pepper Market Crisis: Failure of Corner Attempt," *Glasgow Herald,* February 8, 1935, accessed March 24, 2018, https://news.google.com/newspapers? nid=2507&dat=19350208&id=_KdAAAAAIBAJ&sjid=haUMAAAAIBAJ&pg= 3325,5550510&hl=en; M. Ha, "Chinese Businesses Trying to Overtake Pepper Market: VN Pepper Association," Vietnam Net Bridge, August 14, 2017, accessed March 24, 2018, http://english.vietnamnet.vn/fms/business/183460/chinese -businesses-trying-to-overtake-pepper-market—vn-pepper-association.html.

16. "Growers Hope MIP on Pepper Will Block Dumping of Vietnam Variety," *New Indian Express,* November 8, 2017, accessed March 24, 2018, http:// cms.newindianexpress.com/states/karnataka/2017/dec/08/growers-hope-mip -on-pepper-will-block-dumping-of-vietnam-variety-1721798.html.

17. *Nedspice Farmers Partnership Programme Update 2015,* Nedspice, accessed March 24, 2018, www.nedspice.com/upload/docs/NFPP_update_May_2015.pdf.

Chapter 5

1. Gardiner Harris, "F.D.A. Warns against Use of Popular Cold Remedy," *New York Times,* June 16, 2009, accessed March 24, 2018, https://www.nytimes .com/2009/06/17/health/policy/17nasal.html; "Matrixx Recalls Zicam Nasal Cold Products," Associated Press, June 24, 2009, accessed March 24, 2018, https://www.webcitation.org/query?url=http%3A%2F%2Fwww.forbes.com%2F feeds%2Fap%2F2009%2F06%2F24%2Fap6581515.html&date=2009-06-25.

2. H. Stone and J. L. Sidel, *Sensory Evaluation Practices,* third edition (San Diego, CA: Elsevier Academic Press, 2004).

3. An inexpensive human genetics test paper set including PTC test papers and sodium benzoate are available from scientific and medical supply houses such as Ward's Science in Rochester, New York. Item # 6320100.

4. In cases where the phantom smell is unpleasant (such as burned, foul, spoiled, rotten, moldy) it is called *cacosmia*.

5. Aroma wheels for beer, cheese, cigars, chocolate, coffee, fragrance, honey, maple syrup, olive oil, tequila, whisky, and even body odor have been developed. See, for example, "Flavour Wheels," *Whiskey Science* (blog), July 11, 2011, accessed March 24, 2018, http://whiskyscience.blogspot.ca/2011/07/flavour -wheels.html.

6. The perception of sweetness varies depending on sourness. A small amount of sugar (¼ teaspoon) in a glass of water tastes sweet. If you add some lemon juice, it tastes less sweet. Wine makers are expert at balancing sweetness with other flavors so that even wine containing residual sugar does not taste sweet.

7. A humorous taste-smell experiment is viewable online: https://www .youtube.com/watch?v=VuR6QuWrHrc.

8. Aromas affect other sensory perceptions. See "Fragrance Development," Shiseido, accessed March 24, 2018, https://www.shiseidogroup.com/rd/development/ perfume.html.

9. Pepper spray, a defensive weapon used to incapacitate humans (or bears, bear spray) for twenty minutes or more, works by exposure of capsaicin aerosols to the mucous membranes in the eyes, nose, throat, and esophagus causing extreme pain and discomfort without damage. Although concentrated capsaicin is a toxic compound, chili peppers do not have sufficient concentrations to be harmful to humans. It is interesting that birds lack the TRPV1 receptor, and thus are impervious to the effects of capsaicin.

10. Capsaicin is $C_{18}H_{27}NO_3$; Piperine is $C_{17}H_{19}NO_3$.

Chapter 6

1. One of the three dams forming the Idukki reservoir was designed by SNC Lavalin, a Canadian engineering company. The Idukki Dam was financed with loan guarantees and grants from the Canadian government in 1973. The dam is 168 meters tall, one of the highest dams in Asia. The Idukki reservoir has an area of sixty square kilometers.

2. J. Janick et al., "A History of Grafting," Purdue University, February 9, 2009, accessed March 24, 2018, https://hort.purdue.edu/newcrop/janick-papers/ c09.pdf.

3. ICAR has made a video about their column method. See "Intensifying Black Pepper Productivity," ICAR, March 1, 2015, accessed March 24, 2018, https://www.youtube.com/watch?v=hMsFVLyPkNM.

4. Oleoresin manufacture not only concentrates the oleoresins, it also concentrates harmful materials that may have been in the original light pepper feedstock.

FDA-mandated tests for oleoresins include the presence of residual pesticides, aflatoxin, ochratoxin, yeast, mold, and bacteria such as *E. coli* and *Salmonella*.

Chapter 7

1. Kenji Hirasa and Mitsuo Takemasa, *Spice Science and Technology* (New York: Marcel Dekker, 1998).

2. Researcher and inventor Shigenori Ohta used eleven taster panels to evaluate the perceived saltiness of prepared salt solutions with and without pepper. See S. Ohta, *Shokuhin chomiron* (Tokyo: Saiwai Shobo Company, 1976). US patent #6,974,597 B2 was granted to Shigenori Ohta and his collaborators for a method to enhance the salty taste of foods that contain salt.

3. Petrels have been hunted and eaten by coastal dwellers since prehistoric times. Commonly known as mutton birds, the sooty shearwater (*Puffinus griseus*) is still harvested and sold in New Zealand. Icelanders eat *lundi*, the common Atlantic puffin (*Fratercula arctica*) smoked or boiled.

4. Pavithra Vani Karsha and O Bhagya Lakshmi, "Antibacterial Activity of Black Pepper (*Piper nigrum* Linn.) with Special Reference to Its Mode of Action on Bacteria," *Indian Journal of Natural Products and Resources* 1, no. 2 (2010): 213.

5. M. Nicolič, D. Stojkovič, J. Glamočlija, et al., "Could Essential Oils of Green and Black Pepper Be Used as Food Preservatives?," *Journal of Food Science and Technology* 52, no. 10 (2015), https://www.researchgate.net/publication/273906151_Could_essential_oils_of_green_and_black_pepper_be_used_as_food_preservatives.

6. S. Shobana and K. Akhilender Naidu, "Antioxidant Activity of Selected Indian Spices," in *Prostaglandins, Leukotrienes and Essential Fatty Acids* 2, no. 2 (2000): 107–10, https://ac.els-cdn.com/S095232789990128X/1-s2.0-S095232789990128X-main.pdf?_tid=spdf-624d9ed4-90a6-4034-93ca-3557e800ffcb&acdnat=1519920354_f420929aa58b4fce074ee1c730a1e405.

7. Karan Chawala, Taraneh Tofighi, Arnav Agarwal, et al., "A Global Comparison between Brand-Name and Generic Drugs," *Indian Journal of Pharmacy Practice* 7, no. 3 (July–September 2014): 23–28, http://www.ijopp.org/sites/default/files/10.5530ijopp.7.3.6.pdf.

8. Z. Hu, X. Yang, P. C. Ho, S. Y. Chan, P. W. Heng, E. Chan, W. Duan, H. L. Koh, and S. Zhou, "Herb-Drug Interactions: A Literature Review," *Drugs* 65, no. 9 (2005): 1239–82.

9. Zoheir Damanhouri and Aftab Ahmad, "A Review on the Therapeutic Potential of *Piper Nigrum L.* (Black Pepper): The King of Spices," *Journal of Medicinal and Aromatic Plants* 3, no. 3 (2014). https://www.omicsonline.org/open-access/a-review-on-therapeutic-potential-of-piper-nigrum-l-black-pepper-the-king-of-spices-2167-0412.1000161.pdf.

10. Lokraj Subedee, R. N. Suresh, M. K. Jayanthi, et al., "Preventive Role of Indian Black Pepper in Animal Models of Alzheimer's Disease," *Journal of Clini-*

cal and Diagnostic Research 9, no. 4 (2015). https://www.ncbi.nlm.nih.gov/pmc/articles/PMC4437082/.

11. Touqeer Ahmed, Ghazala Iqbal, Anila Iqbal, Aamra Mahboob, and Mahpara Farhat, "Memory Enhancing Effect of Black Pepper in the AlCl3 Induced Neurotoxicity Mouse Model Is Mediated through Its Active Component Chavicine," *Current Pharmaceutical Biotechnology* 17, no. 11 (2016): 962–73, doi: 10.2174/1389201017666160709202124.

12. J. E. Rose and F. M. Behm, "Inhalation of Vapor from Black Pepper Extract Reduces Smoking Withdrawal Symptoms," *Drug Alcohol Dependence* 34, no. 3 (1994): 225–29.

13. L. Rofes, V. Arreola, A. Martin, and P. Clave, "Effect of Oral Piperine on the Swallow Response of Patients with Oropharyngeal Dysphagia," *Journal of Gastroenterology* 49, no. 12 (2014): 1517–23.

14. P. B. Yaffe, M. Power Coombs, C. Doucette, M. Walsh, and D. Hoskin, "Piperine, an Alkaloid from Black Pepper, Inhibits Growth of Human Colon Cancer Cells Via G1 Arrest and Apoptosis Triggered by Endoplasmic Reticulum Stress," *Molecular Carcinogenesis* 54, no. 10 (2015): 1070–85, doi: 1002/mc.22176.

15. "Piperine Multiplies the Strength of Many Supplements and Drugs," *The Delano Report*, December 27, 2009, http://www.delano.com/blog/?p=70; Inshad Ali Khan, Zahid Mehmood Mirza, Ashwani Kumar, Vijeshwar Verma and Ghulam Nabi Qazi, "Piperine, a Phytochemical Potentiator of Ciprofloxacin against *Staphylococcus aureus*," *Antimicrobial Agents and Chemotherapy* 50, no. 2 (2006): 810–12, http://aac.asm.org/content/50/2/810.full, doi:10.1128/AAC.50.2.810–812.2006.

16. See "Efficacy of *Piper nigrum* (Piperaceae) Extract for Control of Insect Defoliators of Forest and Ornamental Trees, *The Canadian Entomologist* 139, no. 4 (2007): 513–22, https://doi.org/10.4039/n06-040.

Chapter 8

1. "NCDEX in a Fix over Order to Destroy 900 t of Pepper," *The Hindu*, August 19, 2013, accessed March 25, 2018, http://www.thehindu.com/business/Industry/ncdex-in-a-fix-over-order-to-destroy-900-t-of-pepper/article5038831.ece.

2. Final Rule on Foreign Supplier Verification Programs, FDA, May 11, 2017, accessed March 25, 2018, https://www.fda.gov/downloads/Food/Guidance Regulation/FSMA/UCM502160.pdf.

3. CODEX Alimentarius, accessed March 25, 2018, http://www.fao.org/fao-who-codexalimentarius/en/.

4. *Risk Profile: Pathogens and Filth in Spices*, FDA document, January 17, 2018, accessed March 25, 2018, https://www.fda.gov/downloads/Food/FoodScience Research/RiskSafetyAssessment/UCM581362.pdf.

5. "Identification and Prevention of Adulteration," ASTA, March 29, 2017, accessed March 25, 2018, www.astaspice.org/download/10441.

6. "Pepper (*Piper nigrum L.*), Whole or Ground—Specification—Part 1: Black Pepper," ISO Online Browsing Platform, 1998, accessed March 25, 2018, https://www.iso.org/obp/ui/#iso:std:iso:959:-1:ed-2:v1:en.

7. "Pepper (*Piper nigrum L.*), Whole or Ground—Specification—Part 2: Black Pepper," ISO Online Browsing Platform, 1998, accessed March 25, https://www.iso.org/obp/ui/#iso:std:iso:959:-2:ed-2:v1:en.

8. "Malaysian Standard for Pepper," True Ceylon Spices, October 11, 2016, accessed March 25, 2018, http://www.trueceylonspices.com/wp-content/uploads/Malaysian-Standard-for-Pepper.pdf.

9. Lim How Pin, "Sarawak Pepper Still a World-Renowned Brand," *Borneo Post Online*, March 31, 2017, accessed March 25, 2018, http://www.theborneopost.com/2017/03/31/sarawak-pepper-still-a-world-renowned-brand/.

Chapter 9

1. Peppercorns can also be cracked by putting them between two silicone pastry mats and bashing them a few times with a rolling pin.

2. Anton Steeman, "Developments in Disposable Spice Grinders," Best in Packaging, September 4, 2011, accessed March 25, 2018, https://bestinpackaging.com/2014/09/04/developments-in-disposable-spice-grinders/.

Selected Bibliography
and Web Resources

Books

Gantzer, Hugh, and Colleen Gantzer. *Spicestory*. New Delhi: Niyogi Books, 2015.

Hirasa, Kenji, and Mitsuo Takemasa. *Spice Science and Technology*. New York: Marcel Dekker, 1998.

Nair, Prabhakaran. *Agronomy and Economy of Black Pepper and Cardamom: The "King" and "Queen" of Spices*. London: Elsevier, 2011.

Kurlansky, Mark. *Cod: A Biography of the Fish That Changed the World*. New York: Penguin, 1998.

Kurlansky, Mark. *Salt: A World History*. New York: Penguin, 2002.

McFadden, Christine. *Pepper: The Spice That Changed the World*. Bath, UK: Absolute Press, 2012.

Partharasi, V. A., B. Chempakam, and T. J. Zachariah, eds. *Chemistry of Spices*. Cambridge, MA: CABI, 2008.

Peter, K. V. *Handbook of Herbs and Spices*. Boca Raton, FL: CRC Press, 2001.

Ravindram, P. N. *Black Pepper: Piper Nigrum*. Boca Raton: CRC Press, 2005.

Shaffer, Marjorie. *Pepper: A History of the World's Most Influential Spice*. New York: St. Martin's Press, 2013.

Turner, Jack. *Spice: The History of a Temptation*. New York: Vintage Books, 2005.

Web Resources

American Spice Trade Association. http://www.astaspice.org/

Canadian Spice Association. http://www.canadianspiceassociation.com/

ICAR, Indian Institute of Spices Research. http://www.spices.res.in/

International Pepper Community. http://www.ipcnet.org/n/

John Munro, University of Toronto. https://www.economics.utoronto.ca/munro5/SPICES1.htm

Gernot Katzer's Spice Pages. http://gernot-katzers-spice-pages.com/engl/index.html
Nedspice. http://www.nedspice.com/
Spices Board of India. http://indianspices.com/
Sarawak Department of Agriculture. http://www.doa.sarawak.gov.my/modules/
    web/pages.php?mod=webpage&sub=page&id=138
US FDA Food Pages. https://www.fda.gov/Food/default.htm

Index